# LIVING
## *from the*
# INSIDE
# OUT

*How to Get*

*to the Heart of*

*Everything that Matters*

JEAN-MARIE HAMEL, PH.D.

HARMONY BOOKS

NEW YORK

Published by Harmony Books, New York, New York.
Member of the Crown Publishing Group,
a division of Random House, Inc.
www.crownpublishing.com

HARMONY BOOKS is a registered trademark and the Harmony
Books colophon is a trademark of Random House, Inc.

Printed in the United States of America

Design by Chris Welch

Library of Congress Cataloging-in-Publication Data
Hamel, Jean-Marie.
Living from the inside out : how to get to the heart of everything that
matters / Jean-Marie Hamel.—1st ed.
Includes bibliographical references and index.
(hardcover)
1. Self-actualization (Psychology). I. Title.
BF637.S4H34 2004
158.1—dc22        2003027499

ISBN 1-4000-5274-2

10  9  8  7  6  5  4  3  2  1

First Edition

*For Sandi and Bill—*
*With love, honor, and gratitude*

# CONTENTS

# PREFACE

*I know of no more encouraging fact than the unquestionable*
*ability of man to elevate his life by conscious endeavor.*

—HENRY DAVID THOREAU

What are we human beings capable of? Who are we really? How can we be true to ourselves and enjoy a purposeful life? These questions have danced through my mind for as long as I can remember.

The dancing stopped sometime in my midtwenties when I became preoccupied with building what I thought was a secure life. By my late twenties I had managed to adorn my universe with all the trappings of stability and success: a respectable husband, a beautiful home, a career in the family business, and memberships galore in exclusive clubs. The only thing missing from all this splendor was *me*. Despite a monolithic outflow of energy and multiple commitments, I had constructed a life with no one in it—a path with no purpose, a frame with no picture.

Then the questions returned, more insistent than before, and consolidated into one heartfelt inquiry: *How can we enjoy inner fulfillment as well as outer achievement?* In the years that followed, the answer to that question became more evident and provided a clear-cut distinction between "essence" and "form." As my understanding of their interplay deepened, the tapestry it formed became the book you now hold in your hands.

In one sense, it lays the groundwork for increased inner awareness and useful outer applications. At the same time, it presents a practical way to enhance your self-knowledge, let go of what no longer serves you, manifest more of what honors you, and live a more authentic life. In joining both, you move ever closer to the heart of all that matters—the person amidst the splendor, the purpose of the path, the picture in the frame.

*Living from the Inside Out* is based on spiritual principles culled from the world's sacred traditions. Foremost among them is a call for attentiveness to soul—the all-knowing intelligence that resides in us all, regardless of race, creed, color, circumstance, condition, or environment. Although recognized by various names such as true self, authentic nature, divine core, formless essence, natural knowing, seed of God, sacred being, inner self, infinite spirit, unconditional loving, and unmanifested consciousness, this timeless essence is who we truly are. The soul, a vital though invisible part of us, is naturally loving and accepting and connects us to our source, a constant fount of creativity. When we give authority to it, the mind and emotions begin to serve our true purpose in life, awakening within us a sense of wholeness.

Whatever your particular spiritual orientation may be—or may not be—make this book your own. If certain words or phrases are not useful to you, substitute terms that are. For instance, if the word *spirit* or *God* causes you to contract inside, replace it with a word that evokes expansion, such as *freedom* or *oneness*. In general, treat this material in the same way you conduct your life: focus more on what is effective and less on what is not. If a suggestion assists you, use it; if it doesn't, let it go. All the while, pay close attention to your heart's desire, striving for ever more growth, expansion, awareness, and upliftment.

May you awaken to the sacred part of yourself and live in the world as the person you were destined to be. Blessings to you on your journey!

—JEAN-MARIE HAMEL,
Santa Barbara, CA,
February 2004

# INTRODUCTION

*The destiny of man is in his own soul.*

—HERODOTUS

A relationship with our soul is a gift we give ourselves. A celebration of the heart, it transforms ordinary situations into extraordinary delights. Like anything that engages the heart, it heightens our awareness, vulnerability, and compassion; yet because it is rooted in spirit, it also ignites an appreciation of the sacred within us. Respect, acceptance, and trust are therefore required, as is unflagging support and enormous courage. Day by day this relationship showers us with blessings, inviting us to come present in the moment, turn our gaze inward, listen to our deepest truths, and create our lives from the inside out.

One woman describes her soulful connection in these words:

On my best days, I am grateful for my opportunities and laugh at myself regularly. Cherishing all of life, I know I can use everything it presents as a way to further my progress instead of automatically assuming it's out to stop me. I recognize the world as a reflection of my thoughts, feelings, and behaviors, all of which I strive to take responsibility for. I am in my element when I listen to my stillness, face my real and imagined dragons, and slay them one by one. Then I smile from deep inside, privileged to distinguish my illusions from reality and allow the sacred intelligence within me to take charge of manifesting my life.

On my worst days, I'm within a hairsbreadth of joining the ranks of the "walking wounded," who react harshly to life, out of conditioned patterns long outdated. I expect someone else to provide a happily-ever-after wave of the wand, banishing my fears and worries. I judge and blame others for my personal insecurities and inconsiderate behaviors.

Fortunately, I've learned to recognize these attempts to control events by living my life through others. I can tell when I'm disconnecting from my essence, giving away my power, and refusing to strive for my highest potential. Since I cherish my freedom, upon noticing these behaviors I whisper words of encouragement to myself and move forward once again.

Most people want to connect to who they truly are, so they can experience peace and fulfillment and live a purposeful life. But too often this yearning remains unanswered. Psychologists' offices are booked solid, personal growth seminars are filled to capacity, and rarely does an advice column go unread. More-over, research studies reveal that fifteen million Americans are clinically depressed. To ease our pain, we disengage further from ourselves by turning to quick fixes: antidepressants con-stitute a multimillion-dollar industry, alcohol is consumed to excess, cocaine is the number one selling retail product, and material goods are purchased at such an astounding rate that 60 percent of Americans now carry credit card debt.

Why do we have such difficulty establishing a meaningful connection with ourselves? For one thing, Madison Avenue has hardwired us to believe that if we have the object of our dreams, we will be fulfilled: if we own the perfect car, we will attract the romance we deserve; if we use the proper tooth-paste, we will be sexy beyond belief; if we wear the right clothes, we will be loved like never before; and once we have the right relationship, we will be whole and complete. In response, we have come to expect that external accoutrements will bring us the inner experiences we desire. According to this plan, individuals with all the "right" possessions ought to be happy. But instead, many feel disappointed, hurt, and betrayed.

In letting material possessions determine our priorities, we forfeit our vitality, give up our personal power, and become enslaved, immersed in a lifestyle instead of designing a dedi-cated life. Rather than us owning our possessions, *they* end up owning *us* and running our day-to-day existence. As anyone in bondage to material trappings will tell you, they make dreadful masters.

Advertising, however, is not the only culprit. We've also been programmed by Hollywood and our own early childhood conditioning to believe that if we adopt certain roles and behavioral standards we will be socially accepted. Desperate for a sense of belonging, we learned the rules early on: "The one with the most toys in the end gets the thumbs-up," "Be somebody important," "Money can buy you admission to your crowd of choice," "Triumph at all costs," "Fame is the key to glory," "Be perfect," "A partner is the answer to your prayers." But in trying to win at this game, we identified with someone else's script, overrode our own instincts and wishes, and ended up feeling abandoned and lonely. No one told us about the importance of "belonging" first to ourselves.

The problem is that we have been going after *symbols* and *images,* which cannot impart the qualities we truly desire. Automobiles do not make us romantic, toothpaste does not make us sexy, clothes do not make us lovable, partnerships do not make us complete, and borrowed standards of conduct do not pave the way to meaningful relationships. Symbols and images are external forms devoid of essence, and as such they cannot provide fulfillment. When our fascination with them fades, as it must, so does the enjoyment they may have temporarily provided.

Typically, a craving for symbols or images will arise when we are not in contact with our essence. Out of touch with the soul's accepting nature, we may launch forth on buying sprees or undergo cosmetic surgery hoping to nourish ourselves with approval from the outside. Disconnected from our core's link to divinity, we may run for president of an organization, secretly longing to boost our sense of value. But recognition streaming our way in the wake of these missions invariably proves disappointing, because there seems never to be enough of it. Indeed, no amount of approval or esteem from the outside world can satisfy the underlying craving for *self*-acceptance and *self*-worth.

The pursuit of symbols and images epitomizes creation from the "outside in." Such an approach to life is doomed from the start because it focuses on external *forms* and fails to engage our *essence*. Perhaps you have been on this path and become a stranger to yourself and your innermost desires. Or maybe you've experienced excitement early in the quest, only to find it ephemeral and unfulfilling.

A far more rewarding approach is to start from the *inside,* using self-investigation to uncover your soul qualities and letting *these* create the outer form. This two-step method results in a fulfilling creation that, like a good piece of chocolate, has a rich, gooey center (essence) and an outer shell (form). It is then possible to opt solely for inner happiness or worldly acquisitions . . . but why deprive yourself? A life manifested from the inside out is not an either-or proposition. You can have the best of *both* worlds. You can relax into being yourself *and* enjoy material possessions.

Starting from the inside yields other benefits as well. For one, authenticity is not sacrificed; you get to dedicate your efforts to the expression of your true self. For another, frustration decreases because rather than searching madly for gratifying experiences, you can simply allow for them—after all, their appearance is something your divine essence excels in. In addition, your interactions with others will reflect your alignment with your soul. The better acquainted you become with this all-powerful and wise intelligence, the more people you'll find mirroring back your connection with it.

The day you realize that all your thoughts, feelings, behaviors, and relationships originate inside of you, you'll begin cleaning up the inner clutter of conditioning so you can manifest a gratifying adventure on the sea of life. Once cleared of restrictive programming, you'll be able to pilot your own boat through the sometimes calm, sometimes tempestuous waters— course-correcting as needed, yet continually relishing the journey toward your soul's destination.

This book emerged from the experiences of hundreds of men and women who unraveled the mystery of human potential and spiritual awareness: *we can be who we are and have what we want, but we've been going about it backwards.* Part I provides simple techniques for exploring your true self. Part II presents guidelines for manifesting your desires from the inside out. Both procedures actively foster new, more expansive perceptions and relationships.

In seeking to befriend your soul, remember that this essential ingredient is already within you. To engage its participation in creating a more rewarding life, add courage and a heart willing to open one more time than it closes. Then cast off on your course to soul awareness . . . and ports of call you have visited only in dreams.

# PART I
# STEPPING INSIDE

*This above all: To thine own self be true;*

*And it must follow as the night the day,*

*thou canst not then be false to any man.*

—WILLIAM SHAKESPEARE

I magine that you are a spiritual being who has chosen to come to earth in a physical body to learn lessons for your continued growth. Actually picture yourself as this being engaged in a variety of human adventures. Notice how multi-dimensional you are: while your body, mind, and emotions bring you information about the physical, mental, and feeling dimensions of life, your soul is relaying important details about who you are spiritually, what this growth curve looks like, and how to express more of your creative potential.

If you have difficulty envisioning your soul, think of it as a seed of God that was planted at your core before you were born. Just as an apple tree emerges from a tiny seed, we grow from the seed of unconditional love, and we become human, a word that in Sanskrit translates as "God-man." As is true of the tree, we are created and in turn we create, giving of our harvest. For guidance we need only seek the divinity at our core, which will link us directly to our all-knowing and all-powerful source, its creator.

Like a precious gift wrapped inside a decorative box, your soul is the finest part of you: it loves unabashedly, accepts unrestrictedly, understands completely, and serves your best interest unconditionally. Unlike the best tangible asset, your soul is everlasting.

As vital as the soul is, few of us are acquainted with this part of ourselves. We get so caught up in cravings, hurts, and expectations that we forget to "check in" and find out who we really are. Investigators of the spiritual dimension report that the soul has a unique nature. They note that this authentic essence lives in the present moment, rather than dwelling on the past or projecting into the future. It accepts all circumstances, without wishing they were different. It judges neither right nor wrong, but instead operates impersonally, provides direction, and revels in shared discoveries. In addition, the soul embodies not only love, acceptance, and understanding, but the equally expansive qualities of freedom, truth, joy, peace, cooperation, creativity, enthusiasm, and humor—all of which uplift human consciousness. Never do you have to venture outside yourself or depend on exterior circumstances to experience them—they are always at your beck and call.

To encounter your formless essence, you can track any of these qualities inward to its point of origin. Or you can engage in meditation, contemplation, or inner attunement. Some people access their souls while surrounded by beauty or immersed in a natural setting. However your meeting takes place, treat it as a life-changing event, a chance to relax and put your natural knowing in charge of your well-being. Just as the heart is self-regulating while it circulates blood, sending oxygen and other nutrients through the body, so too is your soul; you can rely on this part of you to make the wisest decisions possible. But whereas the heart does its job masterfully without an introductory meeting, the soul requests one. And try as we might to avoid such an encounter, it will at some point occur.

Psychologist Abraham Maslow, a pioneer in human development, likened the inevitability of a soul meeting to Jonah's fate in the Old Testament account. When God first visits Jonah, the prophet flees, terrified by the Creator's power. In response, he is sacrificed to the sea, swallowed by a great fish, and forced to live in its belly for three days and nights. At last agreeing to answer God's call, Jonah is spit out onto dry land. Maslow concluded that all such getaways are futile, that eventually we must stop and face the divine within us.

Many individuals previously asleep to their fate call this encounter a "dark night of the soul." Actually it is an *awakening,* because they can now remember who they are. Jalal a-Din Rumi, a thirteenth-century Sufi philosopher and poet, sounded this eloquent call, urging us to fully awaken to the soul's presence:

> The breezes at dawn have secrets to tell you, don't go back
>     to sleep,
> You must ask for what you truly want, don't go back to sleep.
> People are going back and forth,

Across the doorsill where two worlds touch,
The door is round and open, don't go back to sleep.

Awakening to your divinity is an unforgettable experience. Some people say it is like opening your eyes and suddenly finding a god or goddess within. Others describe it as an immediate awareness of abundant creative forces inside or a profoundly peaceful reunion. Universally, this awakening marks a point of departure from being *form* driven to being *essence* driven, and it unleashes previously hidden reserves of energy for creating greater health, wealth, and love. You get to feel your authentic nature instead of struggling to fill your life with nonessentials.

An initial meeting with the soul calls for a certain lightness of being. If we come laden with mental, emotional, or behavioral misinformation from our past, we will be impeded in our efforts to receive the truth. After all, perceptions of unworthiness, emptiness, or deficits only predispose us to seeing more of the same illusions rather than awakening to the ever-present abundance at our core. The four chapters that follow help you shift your perspective and cast off these encumbrances so you can engage in what just might be the first great meeting of your life. Along the way, you are likely to discover that what you are seeking is seeking *you*.

# Chapter 1

# SURRENDERING WHO YOU ARE NOT

*What the caterpillar calls the end of the world,*
*the butterfly calls the beginning.*

—ZEN SAYING

aster artists know that surrender is the key to creating anything of enduring value. When Italian artist Michelangelo was asked how he sculpted *David,* he replied he carved away everything that wasn't David. His vision was so clear and unobstructed that he could view this magnificent figure in a block of raw marble and release the excess stone, allowing the form to emerge. Spanish painter Pablo Picasso voiced a similar observation when he said, "Every act of creation begins with an act of destruction." You too can release what no longer serves you and then rise to your magnificence.

People setting forth to meet their soul are astonished by the amount of excess inner "baggage" they have accumulated over the years. There are limiting thoughts that drive the mind crazy with self-doubt, crippling emotions that send us on daily roller-coaster spins, and countless disempowering behaviors that sabotage our best efforts toward harmony and well-being. All are components of the personality, adopted early in life either to win love and affection from primary caregivers or to furnish armor against physical or emotional pain. Now, however, these debilitating personality traits are mere camouflage concealing our true spirit, the enduring source of love and protection, so it is best to relinquish them.

"How will I know when I'm ready to give them up?" you might wonder. Thoughts, emotions, and behaviors that restrict your view of the seed of God at your core not only hinder you from experiencing your vast potential but also make you sick and tired—anxiety ridden and sapped of energy. You will know it's time to shed them when you are exhausted from living a sham. At that point you will recognize that engaging in the same thoughts, emotions, and behaviors can only produce the same results as before. Just as Zen practitioners relinquish years of learning in an effort to return to "beginner's mind," you too can part with your camouflage.

"How do I do that?" you might ask. The answer is simple but the way is rarely easy. You can divest yourself of debilitating personality traits first by refusing to give them energy and, second, by replacing them with traits of greater value, filling yourself with qualities from the inside.

In surrendering who you are not, you will be shedding your counterfeit self for a direct experience of your essential essence. As bogus elements fall away, you may feel a twinge of regret at losing them, or embarrassment at having had them. This is only natural. But rather than dwell on your losses, keep moving forward, just as you would if shedding unwanted pounds. Acknowledge that these parts once served you, bless them, and take your next step toward freedom.

Along the way, exercise patience. In nature, where the old is cleared to make way for the new, enduring changes can take more time than fleeting ones. In myths, where birth often begins with death, timetables vary. So prepare for the long haul, hope for a shorter one, and honor your own timing, aware that your reality is being transformed. One day you will regard yourself no longer as a physical organism *of* this world but as a spiritual essence *in* this world.

## LETTING GO OF LIMITING THOUGHTS

Limiting thoughts are toxic. They contaminate us with unwarranted doubts about our potential. These thoughts have us convinced that we are bad, worthless, incapable of loving and being loved. At night they plague us with visions of abandonment and loneliness; by day they assure us that others' motives cannot be trusted.

Rarely do we consider where these thoughts came from. When we do, we discover they were simply opinions or guesses—conclusions drawn from a partial sampling of information. For example, if you see a cat limping along the road, you might conclude it was hit by a passing car, whereas in fact the cat may have stepped on a thorn. Similarly, if your beau flinches when you mention your salary, you might conclude that making more money than he does will cause him to withdraw his affection. An erroneous deduction of this magnitude could have you believing an unfortunate lie and living as if it were the truth.

Most erroneous conclusions are rooted in either false beliefs or punitive judgments. In both instances, prior conditioning has led us to give credence to a distortion of the truth. When your mind is gathering information from unreliable sources, you can easily misinterpret a situation, condemn yourself for having had such a thought, especially if it's negative, and misconstrue the belief or judgment as fact. Your resulting confusion and mistrust can then infect your understanding of other situations, continuing the vicious cycle.

### False Beliefs

Most limiting thoughts emerge from false beliefs like rolled dough cropped by cookie cutters. First, these beliefs mold our perceptions, causing us to see the world as we presume it must be, not as it is. Then we begin interpreting events through these molds. As a result, we become conditioned to a narrow repertoire of perceptions that fail to allow for deviating information, no matter how honest or advantageous it may be.

While growing up on a Louisiana farm, I learned a valuable lesson from my family's pet elephant, Lady Lemah (the family name spelled backward), a lesson I later discovered is also the story of an ancient folktale. Lady Lemah taught me to question my beliefs and become willing to see events from a new perspective. As a baby, any time she was alone in our front yard my father would wrap a heavy chain around one of her back legs and tie it to a large stake anchored deep in the ground. She would rock back and forth, pulling hard to break free. Eventually realizing that she couldn't, she gave up the struggle. Somewhere in her gray matter she must have formed the belief that she was too weak to escape. Then, even as Lady Lemah grew bigger and strong enough to easily snap that chain, she refused to budge, apparently resigned to her presumed fate. It was astonishing to see a huge animal fall victim to a relatively small chain because of an outdated belief about her capabilities. Had Lady Lemah been able to reexamine her beliefs, she would have found the information she was working with had become completely inaccurate. As it was, she continued viewing her present through the cookie-cutter lens of her past.

You, on the other hand, can see yourself differently today than in the past. Endowed with the endless capacity to evaluate your beliefs, you can release those that undermine your best efforts and replace them with beliefs that better express your true nature.

To begin, any time you feel governed by a false belief, own up to it. In acknowledging it, you take authority over it. Here are ten common culprits that may be seriously distorting your picture of reality:

- I am responsible for the feelings of others.
- My past mistakes are unforgivable.
- I am unworthy of pleasure.
- Others' insights are more important than my own.

- I should be perfect at all times.
- I mess up everything I touch.
- People will take advantage of me.
- I must control my family, friends, and coworkers in order to feel safe.
- Nobody understands me.
- I'll never get what I want.

Thoughts and decisions molded by such beliefs are pure fabrications and reflect nothing about who you really are. They can weigh you down with needless burdens, intrude on your natural spontaneity, and keep you plotting and planning for no good reason. So alert yourself to any belief that may be holding you back from adventure and growth.

Start where you are and use the tool of awareness to investigate any personal reactive statements that denote judgments, comparisons, dissatisfaction, unhappiness, fears, or suffering. If you discover any allegations that indicate the composite of a martyr or scapegoat or contain or imply the words *should, ought to,* or *have to,* you've probably identified a false belief. Next, you might want to check for restrictive cultural, organizational, family, religious, community, or peer group positions that you habitually follow.

After identifying a predator, try to recall when you first adopted it. What circumstances gave rise to this perception? Are they still present in your life? Does the belief continue to serve your best interests? If you hold on to this belief, will it give you the results you want? To gain greater awareness and leverage, make a list of the negative effects generated by sustaining this belief as well as a list recognizing the benefits of releasing it. Then honestly ask yourself, "Is it in my highest interest to sacrifice it?" If your answer is a resounding, "Yes!" the next questions are "Am I willing to surrender it?" and "When?"

When you are ready to relinquish your false belief, acknowledge that you are demonstrating the power of conscious choice, tell yourself you will no longer invest energy in the limiting belief, or even give it a second thought. Then replace it with a more honest belief to focus on instead. Examples include the following:

- I am responsible for honoring all parts of myself.
- I am learning from each of my experiences.
- I am worthy and deserve the best.
- My insights are valuable and deserve my attention.
- Who I am is enough.
- My life is a gift and a blessing.
- I am in charge of my responses and reactions.
- The power of love is more fulfilling than the love of power.
- I trust the wisdom of my heart.
- It is up to me to use my energy effectively.

## Punitive Judgments

Other limiting thoughts come from punitive judgments. By-products of false beliefs, these judgments hold us accountable for our convictions, levying a severe sentence. For example, whenever you believe that you or someone else is wrong (bad, incompetent, immoral), this condemnation takes root inside of you, spawning more negativity and criticism. To save face, you may attempt to disown the condemning part of you. Moreover, all thoughts based on that initial judgment will distance you from your loving nature. Many people steeped in punitive judgments become so confused and disoriented that they can see only an occasional glimmer of their own divine essence.

Surrendering negative judgments about yourself can help to put you back in touch with your divine essence and your joy. The first step is to recognize these punitive decrees. They may sound harsh, like the following:

- I am a loser, because I'm not smart (attractive, talented, worldly) enough.
- I'm an ungrateful creep for not acknowledging my parents' assistance.
- I'm a wimp for feeling hurt just because someone turned me down.
- I'm a bad person for breaking my diet with a chocolate ice cream cone.
- I'm a jerk for demanding that others do things my way.
- It's wrong for me to feel jealous just because my coworker got a promotion.
- I deserve punishment for my past behaviors.
- I'm a moron for trying to please others instead of being true to myself.
- Only a fool would feel this anxious about their future.
- I'm an idiot for tuning out my divinity.

The thoughts and decisions that spring from judging yourself can be brutal. You could end up compromising your integrity, settling for less than satisfying relationships, or even refusing to let others please you. So each time you uncover a judgment inside, release it by applying lavish doses of forgiveness. Do your best to open your heart and pardon yourself for the verdict you have delivered.

The more specific you can be, the sooner you will surrender the fake and painful identity you have taken on. For example, tell yourself, "I forgive myself for judging my hurt feelings," "I forgive myself for judging my tendency to place demands on others," "I forgive myself for judging my desire to please others instead of being true to myself," or "I forgive myself for forgetting that I am divine."

Forgiving ourselves for judging others is equally healing. Think of a time when someone important to you failed to live up to your expectations. Did you immediately form a negative opinion about them? If so, how did you feel afterward? Most people feel small and constricted after condemning others for their behavior.

My client Carla is a case in point. When Carla was a young child, her father beat her with his belt if she spilled juice at the table, berated her in front of friends, and frequently told her she was "no good." Consequently, she grew up fearing and hating him for his cruelty. Although he died when she was sixteen years old, her judgments of him did not. To the contrary, with each verdict she passed she had built an imaginary wall around herself that was intended to protect her from anyone who might hurt her, but instead, it kept the real enemy—Carla, as self-appointed judge, jury, and jailer—within. Her hostility permeated all her relationships. Seeing how her father was running her life from the grave, I encouraged Carla to forgive him, not for his sake but for her own. As part of her assignment, she agreed to write a personal story, forecasting how her life would be if she continued holding on to her resentments. When she read it aloud to me, tears rolled down her cheeks as she denoted in detail the disastrous course she was navigating. Instead of realizing a bright future, her account entailed more pain, sorrow, and suffering. Trembling, she finally recognized the tragic reality of her punitive judgments.

Next, she wrote a different story, predicting the process and outcome of her life if she released her condemning judgments. She sat up straight and read this version with a gleam in her eyes and a smile on her face. Although both stories had the same beginning, the endings were radically different. Instead of a tragedy, the second version transformed into a love story. The difference between the two renditions was astounding and enough to convince Carla to change course. She opted for victory and began, one by one, releasing her judgments. Then she filled those once angry and painful places with compassion, giving herself the love her father had been incapable of providing. Although it wasn't easy, Carla's willingness to surrender her past grievances initiated the healing process. Her resolution allowed hidden blessings to be revealed—strengthening her character, and enhancing her future.

Carla's story suggests that although it may be instinctive and understandable to judge an abuser, we cannot afford the luxury of this negative thought. The good news is that forgiving ourselves for passing such judgments alleviates our suffering. At the same time, it puts us back in touch with the parts of ourselves we have disowned and draws us closer to our loving nature. Statements representing this type of forgiveness include the following:

- I forgive myself for judging my parents for not loving me the way I wanted to be loved.
- I forgive myself for judging women as weak and timid.
- I forgive myself for judging men as cruel and controlling.
- I forgive myself for judging God as unjust and uncaring.

## RELEASING CRIPPLING EMOTIONS

Just as some thoughts restrict our view of our spiritual nature, so too do certain emotions. On their own, emotions are not debilitating; they are simply "energy in motion" passing through the body. These emotions do not mean anything; we have invented their meaning based on past circumstances. If we simply observe them, they take no strong hold on us. But should we ascribe personal meaning to this energy, it becomes charged and suddenly capable of dominating our lives, at times incapacitating us. We react based on old memories and scare ourselves. We are then at the mercy of our worry, fear, hurt, anger, sadness, jealousy, despair, shame, or other crippling emotion.

While flowing through the body, emotions transmit valuable feedback about our inner landscape, providing us with barometric readings on otherwise imperceptible responses—their nature and intensity, their fluctuations, the buildup and tapering off of near tempests. But once we attribute personal significance to any of these "weather systems," it can stop us in our tracks, rendering us too powerless to be true to ourselves.

We invest energy with meaning when we personalize the triggering event. For example, a client once told me that while she was a child her father rarely spoke to her. "What's wrong with me?" she would ask herself. Because this woman associated communication with loving, she concluded that she must be unlovable. For days on end this thought would sweep her up in whirlpools of emotion she later identified as rejection and brokenheartedness.

How do you deal with the energy of emotions? Do you value the input or take it personally? Do you let your emotions run you? Do they sometimes paralyze you? If so, you can get back on course by neutralizing them and letting them go. My client neutralized her charged emotions when she learned as an adult that her father had seldom spoken to people he spent hours with each day, including his employees. Her new perception allowed her to note that the outward circumstance triggered a recurring inward reaction that was draining her of energy. By "owning up" to the facts, she now took back command. The discovery about her father deactivated her sadness and enabled her to release it.

Giving up a crippling emotion, as well as surrendering obstructive thoughts, calls for awareness, acknowledgment, and action. Awareness denotes perception, discernment, and realization. It enables you to gather information as well as see firsthand the internal condition. Through recognition, the emotion is lured out of hiding and comes to light. All the while, you can observe what's happening.

Confirming and greeting an emotion acknowledges it presence. Denying it only causes it to stay stuck and to continue replaying its drama, over and over like a broken record. Instead, naming it and claiming it rearranges the power base, putting you in charge of the unruly emotion.

Through action, you can consciously release it. The willingness to do it often yields the ability to do so. Simply allow for the emotional energy to pass through you. If a tug-of-war ensues, forgiveness is the key. Or, perhaps like Carla, writing the benefits of discharging it could prove advantageous. The action you take to consciously release it sets you free to once again fill the space with something of greater value and learn from your emotions. This three-step procedure can purge you of the most intractable emotions, such as worry and fear.

## Worry

I grew up in a house of worry. The unspoken family code was, "If you're not worrying, you're not caring." To show how much I cared, I tried to worry more than anyone else. Soon enough, worry had me in its grip. I mistook the resulting tension, distress, and gut-gnawing disturbances for the price of loving. As years passed, the cost soared: my health became increasingly compromised and the return on my investment diminished. Worse, the decision I had made innocently in childhood had escalated into a habit, an obsession, and ultimately an enslavement. I was a worry junkie in constant need of a fix.

Worry beads, worry stones, and worry lines etched on the forehead only hint at the preponderance of worry in our culture. This nervousness, or stress, deposits tension in the body. When it settles in the shoulders, the tension leads to a painful stiff neck; in the stomach, it causes indigestion; in the colon, alternations between constipation and diarrhea; and in the jaw, headaches and temporal mandibular joint dysfunction, better known as TMJ. Over time, the buildup of muscular tension, combined with chemical and biological stress reactions, can lead to exhaustion.

If you often agitate over things that might go wrong, you may well be plagued by worry. To release this emotion, first increase your awareness of it by noticing the part of your body it most frequently inhabits. Observe it without judging it. What does it feel like? What does it sound like? Then, acknowledging its presence, befriend it and invite it to tell you how it got there. While practicing compassionate listening, you may discover that decades ago you chose to invest in this energy because it signified caring, as it did in my household, or because it elicited comforting, soothing, or sympathy from others.

Having identified the meaning you ascribed to worry, see if it serves its purpose today. Ask yourself: "What's the present payoff for my old indulgence in agitation?" "Are the results worth the tension and exhaustion I'm experiencing?" "Is this emotion in charge of me or am I in charge of it?" "If I continue engaging in worry, how will it affect my future?" When you are ready to let go of worry, replace it with something of greater value and thank yourself for caring enough to participate in the process.

The most potent replacement is humor, igniter of happiness, health, and spirit. Many of us worriers take ourselves so seriously that we close our hearts to fun and enjoyment, which rapidly elevates anxiety levels. Since humor and worry can't occupy the same psychological space at the same time, it's our choice as to which one will stay. With compelling motivation, clear intention, and committed action, we can choose to substitute lightheartedness and an occasional belly laugh for worry. To practice the sport, watch a funny movie, read a joke book, keep a folder with your favorite jokes, listen to a recording of your favorite comedian, or visit a comedy club. When we do, our hearts reopen and bless us with joy. Begin and end each day with laughter, and see how quickly your happiness soars.

In terms of health, humor is a proven wonder drug. In 1964, bestselling author Norman Cousins cured himself of a degenerative disease of the connective tissue by self-medicating with laughter in large doses. Since then research groups in the expanding field of psychoneuroimmunology (humor) have acknowledged the positive effects of this natural healer. In 1985, Dillon and Baker discovered that watching a funny video caused levels of an immune system protein to rise in subjects' bodies. In 1989, L. Berk found that stress hormone levels lowered and the number of immune defense cells in the blood increased as a result of laughter. A research group led by H. M. Lefcourt in 1994 determined that laughter increased the activity of certain immune cells known as "natural killer" cells. Additional scientific studies have since shown that humor significantly affects autoimmune and other physiological functions. It reduces tension, boosts energy levels, lowers the heart rate, increases the number of disease-fighting cells, decreases blood pressure, enhances oxygen consumption, suppresses the production of the stress hormone epinephrine, and promotes the release of endorphins, leading to a "natural high."

Humor has also been proven to have a positive psychological influence on children. Children receiving immunizations in a

1995 study by L. Cohen displayed less stress when they watched a funny video of their choice. The children's parents and nurses said they felt less stress during the immunizations, too.

Humor's boost to spirit is reflected in the origins of the word itself. When you separate the word *humor* into its composite parts, you find *hu,* an ancient Sanskrit word meaning God, and *more,* an adjective signifying "to a greater extent or degree." Infusions of humor can rapidly alert you to a new, magnified experience of the spirit at your core. However you go about lightening up, humor and its sidekick laughter are sure to remind you that who you are is lots more fun than the worry cover-up you may have concocted early in life.

### Fear

If worry is a squall, then fear is a typhoon. This emotion wells up instantly, and sometimes with such intensity that it can immobilize us in a heartbeat. But though its force is mighty, its catalyst can be a mere shred of memory.

A client of mine was on a sunset walk with a friend when suddenly a man and his large rottweiler turned the corner and headed in their direction. The woman froze, panic-stricken, as her friend ambled on, undaunted by the dog. Only after the man and his pet strode past them could the woman relax enough to explain her alarm. "As a four-year-old," she told her friend, "I was knocked over by a huge dog, and ever since, I have been terrified of them. My mind stages an attack, fear kicks in, and immediately I'm paralyzed." The sense of personal harm this woman had attributed to this childhood encounter was so pronounced that, at the sight of any large dog, she still became inundated with fear.

I envision the word *fear* as an acronym for "fantasy expectations appearing real." When I'm under the spell of fear, this association helps me remember that I have frightened *myself* by imagining a terrifying outcome. The acronym once brought me to my senses while I was studying for a final exam and suddenly began to dwell on the possibility of failing it, flunking out of school, finding no suitable employment, and becoming a bag lady. In an instant, my mind had leaped from academic work to impoverishment, and I was immobilized by fear.

Fear triggered by the imagination is incapacitating because of the physiological response it elicits. We are endowed with an automatic fight-or-flight response that floods the body with adrenaline in preparation for dealing with danger; however, the nervous system cannot distinguish between a real danger and a fictitious threat. Therefore, whenever your brain registers a fantasized expectation of danger, your body vaults into "hyperalert" mode, primed for peril. In response, you may feel so rattled that you'd sooner freeze than take a chance and risk negative results.

Signs of fear are easy to spot. There may be stomach cramps, sweating, shortness of breath, constricted pupils, tightness of the muscles, or a racing heart. You can safely conclude you are in the grip of fear if you'd rather refrain from loving than risk hurt or rejection, or if you'd sooner resist asking for what you want than gamble on disappointment. You're dancing with fear each time you withhold your truth to avoid possibly losing someone's approval, or refuse to display a special talent out of concern that it might not be "good enough." You're confined by fear if you are reluctant to seek your soul because you are scared of the unknown.

Fear reigns at the center of all violence. It convinces us to believe terrible lies about ourselves such as:

- We are powerless.
- The enemy is outside of us.
- We're not lovable.
- We're all alone.
- We must suffer.
- We must be punished.
- We must seek revenge.

To liberate yourself from these fears or any others, deepen your awareness of it by observing its physiological effects on you. Notice the internal dialogue that is raging inside your head. Then acknowledge the emotion by naming it and admitting that it originates in a fantasy expectation. Based on an outdated and self-imposed standard, you frighten yourself and behave as if it were the truth. It isn't. Stop and ask yourself, "What value do I get from holding on to erroneous rules?" "If I didn't have this fear, what emotion could I entertain instead?" "What might I be missing out on by allowing this fear to govern my life?" When you are ready to risk greater happiness, release the fear by correcting any erroneous information and exchanging the losing scenario for a winning one that celebrates your potential.

A useful replacement for the energy of fear is courage. It is courage that emboldens epic heroes and heroines, from dragon slayers to women in labor, to venture forth despite real or imagined outcomes. Although easier said than done, the trials endured based on the courage of their convictions in turn give birth to a new way of being, or even a new life. In the book *The Power of Myth,* Joseph Campbell, one of the world's foremost authorities on mythology, describes the hero's journey not only as an adventure but as a life lived in self-discovery, which grants one the wisdom and power to serve others. He summons us all to awaken to this journey and to feel the rapture of being alive.

At age eight, I unknowingly accepted a test of my mettle in the face of danger. One hot and muggy July morning, days after my father had purchased a pair of adult brown bears, they escaped and were spotted about two hundred yards from their habitat on our property. Before long, the area was swarming with reporters, TV film crews, and armed deputies haggling over a viable rescue plan. Concerned that someone might harm the bears, I stepped forth, ice cream cone in hand, to rescue them myself. Dressed in navy shorts, a white T-shirt, and thong sandals—hardly bear-grappling attire—I moseyed over to the furry creatures and offered them a lick of my ice cream. They graciously accepted, and with the next lick I began leading them back home. Although the crowd screamed with alarm for my well-being, I remained calmly focused on my mission and, lick by lick, walked the bears all the way home. The next morning, my photograph appeared on the front page of my hometown newspaper with the caption, "A Child Shall Lead Them Home." What the reporter did not know was that the child had no thought of self-sacrifice but had simply followed her heart and kept her mind focused on the task at hand.

While fear can often paralyze us, the gift of courage can generally get us past being stuck.

Many people say their greatest acts of courage are not physical deeds but rather emotional ones—demonstrations of affection, tenderness, and closeness. When vulnerability is at stake, the courage required for emotional intimacy is akin to the boldness needed to enter a swimming pool for the first time. Although some like to jump right in while others prefer to inch in gradually, both expressions of courage lead to the discovery that life can be enormously pleasurable when we are willing to take risks.

Although American author and lecturer Helen Keller was deaf and blind from infancy, she encouraged others to live life to the fullest by moving beyond their self-imposed boundaries and taking risks. She advised, "Avoiding danger is not safer in the long run than outright exposure. Life is either a daring adventure or nothing." But her life wasn't always lived "on purpose." History tells us that at an early age, she was frustrated, unruly, filled with rage, and run by her emotions. It wasn't until her family hired tutor Anne Sullivan that Helen learned to take mental dominion over her emotions and develop a new attitude. Instead of altering her life based on limitations, she consciously chose to construct her life based on courage. As a result, she went to college, wrote ten books, met twelve American presidents, traveled to thirty-nine countries on five continents, learned to read French, German, Greek, and Latin in braille, inspired two Oscar-winning movies, and received the United States Presidential Medal of Freedom, the highest honor a private citizen can receive. By using her mind and emotions to serve her true nature, she inspired a nation and left a worldwide legacy.

It takes courage to access the hero or heroine inside you, to accept healthy challenges, to go where you've never been before, and to dare to be your loving self. But once you've set the adventure in motion, you cannot help but encounter hidden parts of yourself and emerge delightfully transformed.

## GIVING UP DISEMPOWERING BEHAVIORS

To access the soul, it is important to give up not only restrictive mental and emotional patterns, but also behavioral patterns that drain energy and pull the plug on personal power. Disempowering behaviors spin so much chaos into our physical universe that it becomes difficult to move forward. Sapped of vital forces, we wonder how we will ever harness enough energy to wash the dishes stacked in the sink, write the thank-you notes, and pick up the clothes from the floor, much less honor our spiritual commitments to ourselves. We feel worn out and defeated even before we begin. But begin we must, if we are to meet our true selves.

Disempowering behaviors are often deeply ingrained. If you have been habituated to a variety of them, perhaps for decades, you may not realize the stores of energy you're drizzling away. Ask yourself throughout the course of any day if you are getting the results you want, and you will discover how much more energy efficient you can be. To rid yourself of these habits, tune in to them; own up to them; and, stating your desired outcomes, replace the old habits with more empowering ones that will give you a greater return on your energy investments.

Three of the biggest energy drains in daily life are unfinished business, clutter, and addictions. The behaviors that feed such practices use precious resources desperately needed for being who you are and getting what you want. To make room in your life for a creative, energizing relationship with your soul, surrender these ineffectual tactics. Since life abhors a vacuum, fill the empty space with loyal tactics that support your true nature.

## Unfinished Business

Unfinished business encompasses the many endeavors that have been thought about but not yet brought to fruition. There's the mail in your in-basket, the e-mail on your computer, messages on your voice mail, unpaid bills, upcoming deadlines, quarterly taxes, batteries to purchase, or a button to sew on your favorite blouse. Because of the attention you have already given to such endeavors, a portion of your energy field remains committed to them. To reclaim this energy, you must either complete them or declare them complete, and let them go.

For example, if several months ago you started cleaning your garage and stopped after arranging the tools and gardening supplies, the project is continuing to consume your energy. Since it's in full view, serving as a constant reminder of a task requiring your attention, it may be sapping even more energy. One client left a newly initiated fifteen-hundred-piece jigsaw puzzle that she didn't really enjoy doing on her dining room table for two months. In the evenings, she found herself feeling too depleted of ideas to work on the mystery novel she was writing and too tuckered out to play Frisbee with her children. Only when she officially gave up on the puzzle, had disassembled the interlocked corners, put all the pieces back in the box, and gave it to a friend did she spring back to life in the evenings.

As you free yourself of unfinished business, your vitality will return. And the more you stop perpetuating the habit of letting it linger in your life, the closer you will come to achieving your heart's desires. After homing in on this behavior and acknowledging the part it plays in your life, assess its value and consequence. Ask yourself if it is producing the results you want. If not, substitute a more energy-efficient habit, such as completion. Once you begin completing your undertakings or declaring them complete, you will be sailing ahead at your own pace, no longer subject to wind drag.

## Clutter

Items that don't belong where they are, or the way they are, establish an "open loop" tugging on your attention. An environment marked by disorder and disarray reduces productivity, diminishes mental clarity, heightens aggravation, and intensifies anxiety. Clutter, in other words, wears us down physically, mentally, and emotionally. When we allow an exterior area to be filled to the brim with antiquated jumble, it also squelches precious space in our interior world. It keeps us from exposing our dreams to air and discovering who we really are; more often than not, it binds us to memories of who we once thought we were.

If you have been besieged by clutter demons for quite some time, you may not realize their impact. Physically, mounds of clutter may be obscuring your vision and hampering your ability to perform at your best. Are you frequently unable to find things? Do you derive little joy from your surroundings? If so, it's probably time to roll up your sleeves and address the mess head-on.

Mentally, these demons may be contributing to fuzzy thinking or spells of forgetfulness. Do you have difficulty maintaining your focus? Have you ever dashed to the kitchen and arrived oblivious to your reason for being there? If you have, eliminate the clutter. Organizing your living space will help relieve you of excessive mental chaos.

Clutter's emotional tyranny can be even more devastating. Do you sometimes feel overwhelmed and incompetent? Are you occasionally flooded with other outdated feelings, such as lack of confidence or motivation? If so, clear out the archival debris and renovate your environment. Let go of outgrown clothing, broken furniture, old magazines, once-sentimental knickknacks, and stacks of paper that no longer represent who you are and where you are going.

Next, kick the clutter habit altogether and replace it with a more energy-efficient behavior, such as recycling. When you recycle, your litter can become someone else's treasure. Better yet, the more you simplify your surroundings, the more revved up you'll be to retrieve your dreams from the nooks and crannies they've slipped into.

## *Addictions*

Addictions hook our energy to counterfeit sources of fulfillment. An addiction—whether to food, overspending, overworking, computers, TV, sex, alcohol, nicotine, gambling, drugs, or any of a thousand obsessive routines—leaves a deadening force in its wake. It barks commands at us, and we follow in lockstep, mindlessly expending vital energy.

Many addictive behavior patterns are rooted in prior emotional disturbances that at the time were so upsetting we sought to distance ourselves from our feelings. Little did we know that we were also distancing ourselves from our soul. We knew only that the "fix" made the pain go away, if only temporarily. When it returned, so did our search for the magic potion—or perhaps a stronger one, with greater numbing capacity.

These behaviors are now wreaking havoc in new contexts, perpetuating dependencies, energy leaks, and feelings of powerlessness. For example, upon hearing angry words you might revert to a childhood habit of reaching for something sweet, such as a candy bar or a sugary dessert, to quell your anxiety. Although the sugar may offer immediate solace, it cannot help you address the cause of your upset. Nor can it fill you with the kindness and gentleness you are seeking. All it can do is provide instant gratification, engage your energy in a futile search for satisfaction, and add extra pounds. The way out of this conundrum is to give up the addictive behavior and replace it with a more empowering ritual, such as talking sweetly to yourself. While communicating with yourself lovingly, compassionately, and with an understanding heart, you can indeed fill yourself up with sweetness from the inside.

Addiction to alcohol poses the same dilemma but on a grander scale, because alcohol is more physically habituating and destructive. Most people who turn to excessive drinking do so to numb their intense feelings. But without access to these feelings, which can help unveil the root cause for the addiction, habitual drinkers end up in double jeopardy: the cause for their addiction remains unknown yet operative, and they are now plagued with the abuses of alcoholism as well. Those who overcome the addiction, slaking their thirst with spirit rather than bottled spirits, reclaim their energy and find their way home to themselves.

Giving up an addictive behavior of any sort requires an awareness of the habit and where it is leading you, as well as acknowledgment of your underlying feelings, which can direct you to the cause of the problem. Professional help is an option. Also, several well-established programs deal specifically with the treatment and management of addictions.

Be sure to substitute the disempowering behavior with a ritual that gives expression to your inner core. Creative hobbies that capture your interest and provide you with feelings of contentment and delight are excellent replacements as are forms of exercise such as swimming, yoga, tai chi, tennis, golf, and hiking. Your new ritual may in time become a habit, but this one will be healthy. Healthy habits reinforce personal strengths rather than weaknesses, and ultimately lead to enhanced self-esteem. Nourished by the awesome realization that you are more powerful than your addiction, you will begin honoring yourself and, perhaps for the first time, trusting yourself. All the while, great stores of energy will be liberated for creating a relationship with your spirit.

## RESETTING YOUR INNER THERMOSTAT

Expansive thoughts, emotions, and behaviors invigorate the inner environment, but they do not come furnished with holding power. On the contrary, they can pass right through you like weather systems unless you actively contain them.

Here's why. It is as if our inner comfort zone were equipped with a device programmed to restore customary conditions any time they have been altered. Like a household thermostat that compensates for variations in temperature, this inner device automatically counteracts personality changes, ensuring the preservation of old, familiar traits. Consequently, a new personality trait can only take hold if you reset your inner thermostat to account for it and intermittently reinforce the adjusted setting.

To reset your thermostat, follow these guidelines:

- Each time you apply an upgraded thought, emotion, or behavior, ask yourself, "Am I attaining my desired outcome? Is this working for me?" If it is, activate it over and over again.
- Monitor your progress, either on your own or with a trusted friend. Are you experiencing more of your potential? Do you feel freer and more capable of accomplishing your goals? If so, take time to honor your new skills.
- Appreciate your willingness to learn, grow, and expand.

To reinforce your thermostat's new and improved setting, repeatedly remind yourself how well your more expansive personality traits are serving you. For example, if you adopted the new belief "My life is a gift and a blessing," and have begun viewing your life through this lens, recall the sparks of happiness you've been experiencing. Or, if you substituted healthy and nutritious eating for binge eating, appreciate and congratulate yourself. Do this every day. The more you focus on strengthening your new traits, the sooner they will rise to expression on their own and form your new comfort zone.

When we take charge of our inner environment, we start showing up more fully in the world. No longer intent on living from crisis to crisis, we up the ante on our personal truths, our newly softened hearts, our strength and our tenderness, our divinity and our humanity, and our desire to bring goodness and beauty to the world.

After surrendering who you are not, you will be well prepared to leave your old baggage on shore and launch out onto the sea of life in search of your heart's treasure—less defended, perhaps, but more aware of how you operate. Invite your soul on board as captain, and your new thoughts, emotions, and behaviors as crew. This way you can set sail with confidence knowing, in the words of Edward Gibbon, author of *The History of the Decline and Fall of the Roman Empire,* "the winds and waves are always on the side of the ablest navigators."

*Chapter 2*

# OPENING TO WHO YOU ARE

*Be what you is,*
*cuz if you be what you ain't,*
*then you ain't what you is.*
—GUNSLINGER'S EPITAPH,
Boothill Cemetery,
Tombstone, Arizona

An old creation story tells us that in the beginning there was only God but God did not know himself. To learn who he was, he created forms and placed a seed of himself into each one—every rock, every tree, the sun, the moon, every bird, fish, and animal, every man, woman, and child. He then proclaimed: "What you are is my gift to you. What you become is your gift to me."

The forms, once absorbed in their surroundings, assumed they were physical entities having a spiritual experience. And so God learned patience from the rocks, simplicity from the trees, focus from the sun, laughter from the moon, freedom from the birds, playfulness from the fish, ordinariness from the animals, thinking from the men, emotion from the women, and innocence from the children. He recognized these as noble character traits reminiscent of his energy field, but he was perplexed. Something was missing—a force far more powerful than any the forms had taught him.

God let out a long sigh. His breath, filling the forms with bliss, reminded them that they were not physical forms having a spiritual experience but rather seeds of God having a physical experience. Immediately, love stirred deep within them, and the more they opened to their essence and expressed that love, the faster it grew.

God now knew of his loving nature, whereupon his bewilderment turned to joy. To celebrate the blessing of finally knowing all of himself, he expanded with peaceful wisdom—and so, too, did the forms. From that day on, whenever they felt lonely or lost, the forms knew just how to come home to themselves.

## THE NATURE OF REMEMBERING

You, like all forms of creation, are divine. But perhaps you have overidentified with your thoughts, emotions, or behaviors and forgotten about God's gift to you.

When we human forms forget about the essence at our core, we close ourselves off from our loving nature and lapse into misperceptions, miscommunications, and misunderstandings. Then we place our authority with the personality instead of the soul, and end up worshiping second-rate deities, such as the god of opinion, the god of lust, the god of defensiveness, the god of approval, the god of comparison, the god of despair, the god of force, the god of control, and the god of perfection. Prostrate in this pantheon of lesser gods, we can easily lose our power by believing the illusions flashing back at us about who we are. That's when loneliness and confusion set in.

Have you ever thought that satisfying an urge for recognition would bring you happiness? Have you ever felt so self-righteous that it was impossible to listen to another point of view? Did you ever attempt to exercise control because you didn't know who was in charge of your behavior? Do you try hard to make things happen your way, only to find circumstances getting worse? Did you ever attempt to fill an inner emptiness with outer experiences but discover there were never enough to alleviate the pain? Do you sometimes tell yourself, "If only I had the right relationship," "If only I had the perfect career," "If only my mother had breastfed me," or "If only I were younger (older, prettier, richer) . . . I could stop being disgusted with my life"? If so, you may be trapped in the same exasperating predicament as most people who bow at the feet of personality lords. In remembering who you are, you'll realize that these are gods of deceit and you are actually magnificent and loving.

There are as many ways of remembering our divine essence as there are human seeds of God. All are valuable and deserving of respect. For some people, the turning point arrives unexpectedly, following a physical or emotional shake-up, or a sudden interruption in their ordinary response to life. Others come to it out of a longing for wholeness, or a gnawing sense that with determination they can regain the epicenter of their existence and uncover their purpose. Whether through pain or pleasure, seemingly accidental or deliberate, the experience of remembering God's gift of soul is usually described as a realization that one has been asleep, a dawning of consciousness, an emerging from dormancy—in short, an awakening. Often this event is portrayed not only as an awakening *to* the soul but as an awakening *of* the soul. It is as if the act of remembering our loving nature causes it to rise and shine.

## AWAKENING TO THE SOUL

It is enlightening to awaken to the loving soul. If you have been identifying with your form—your body, mind, and emotions—you are probably accustomed to a certain palette of world colors. But its glow is nothing compared with the shimmering radiance of the soul. This is the brilliant hue that master artist Marc Chagall spoke of when he explained, "In our life there is a single color . . . which provides the meaning of life and art. It is the color of love."

Perhaps you knew this at one time and chose to conceal your gift of love, for fear it might be plundered or looted. Maybe you hid it so well that you lost sight of it. If you did, a game of hide-and-seek might prove astonishing, only this time be the seeker. The virtues of delving beneath surface features are recorded in the following true story I heard while traveling in Asia.

A long time ago, a peace-loving tribe in northern Thailand adorned the center of their prosperous village with their most revered object—a five-foot-tall golden Buddha. Day and night, this sacred statue kept them focused on transcending the bounds of worldly phenomena. Years later, upon hearing of pillaging warlords roving through the countryside, the tribe covered their golden Buddha with mud so it would not be noticed and perhaps stolen. The plan worked. Sure enough, warlords raided the village and left the now earthen figure undisturbed while seizing all the gold and silver they could find, as well as countless objects of great value. But amid the struggle, the villagers lost their lives. Decades later, the village was resettled by a community of peaceful people who began to worship this earthen Buddha. As the village grew, the venerated statue was no longer in its center but on the outskirts, so a group of monks arranged for a crane to move it back to its place of distinction. When the crane hoisted it up, however, the earthen Buddha cracked, sending a jagged fracture down its facade. Alarmed and saddened, the monks prayed for guidance. That night, as a full moon shone down on the earthen Buddha, a bright light glowed from within it. Moved by a profound sense of love, a monk, pick in hand, began chipping away at the statue's exterior and, to his amazement, uncovered a magnificent solid-gold Buddha.

A soul, beckoned by love, comes out of hiding in much the same way. If we think who we are is what we do, we may tend to be overachievers, acquire an excess of credentials, and join prestigious organizations for recognition. At first glance, we are shocked when a chink in the otherwise unbroken surface of our personality reveals it to be only a disguise. Then curiosity sets in, prompting questions similar to Dorothy's in *The Wizard of Oz,* before the good witch, Glinda, tells her "the power" has been inside her all this time. Soon we want to know more, see more, and be more.

Upon witnessing the majesty beneath our loneliness and confusion, we embark on an adventure that can enrich our life forever. This does not mean, however, that the way will always be easy. In fact, reports indicate that it usually entails a combination of agony and ecstasy. As we shed our shield of defenses, we open to the anguish of disillusionment and loss. Although the realizations can be painful, our yearning to experience the liberation of the soul and encounter its magnificence draws us closer to the formless. We marvel at this new sense of self; and the more attention we give it, the bigger it grows, like the radiance of the villagers' Buddha.

Awakening to who you are is life altering in other ways, as well. Instead of looking outside yourself for answers, you'll be turning inward. If as a result of past experiences you associate loving with control and demands, you'll realize that true loving is deeply tender and patient, kind and compassionate. You'll become accountable for your past and present circumstances and feel deserving of a more fulfilling future. Rather than sailing along in blind faith or doubt, you'll have a clear vision of your purpose and direction, having placed your trust in a reality far more faithful than your compass.

Best of all, instead of assuming that life is "happening" to you, you will be directing it, as you would a movie. As its hero or heroine, your part can be as impromptu as Indiana Jones's was in the film *Raiders of the Lost Ark*. When asked, "Who should do it?" Jones replied, "I am the person for the job." When asked, "What are you seeking," he answered, "It is not of this earth." When asked, "How will you do it?" he said, "I don't know . . . I'm making it up as I go." Once you begin taking cues from your essence, you too will be embarking on a series of adventures by merely showing up and experiencing life as it comes. There is enormous freedom in awakening to a spiritual reality greater than our own willpower.

## APPROACHES TO AWAKENING

The word *Buddha* means one who has woken up. Gautama Buddha, the founder of Buddhism, awakened to truth while meditating under a tree on the banks of the Nairangana River in northern India. But to awaken to your divinity you don't have to fly to India or spend days sitting motionless under a tree. You can wake up to the extraordinary in the course of everyday life.

Theoretical physicist Albert Einstein espoused that problems cannot be solved with the same level of consciousness that created them. To move to a higher level of awareness in the midst of an ordinary day, use the following five methods.

### Attunement to Nature

Nature provides an ideal setting for awakening to the soul. While outdoors, listen for the spirit of the wind, trees, the earth, or animals, and you may soon feel your soul stirring in response. Relax and observe the harmonious balance of the great outdoors. Feel the earth beneath your feet and notice how it supports you. Be aware of the natural forces in Mother

Nature's workshop. Or lie on a soft patch of earth and, watching clouds drift across the sky, notice the part of you connecting with the intelligence that guides all of life. Now move beyond the borders of the known world and join the powers of heaven and earth and celebrate the dance of the sacred energies. Transcend any personal concerns and move into the formless from which all forms emanate. Allow yourself to be nurtured and nourished as you yield to the great unknown. Nature's catalyzing forces can spark an immediate sense of a grand plan in which the soul is at one with the majesty of creation.

## Conversations with God

Conversing with God, however you envision this divine loving intelligence, can help you not only become aware of your soul but also glean information from it. Like any good conversationalist, you will want to speak clearly and listen well. Talk as though you were speaking to a friend, a counselor, a corporate partner, a travel companion, or the Creator of the universe, whichever you prefer. Ask for answers to questions, solutions to problems, or simply a sign of God's presence. If the replies you hear are supportive of your growth, you can trust they are coming through the seed of God within you.

Another way to converse with God is through letter writing. Last year I jolted awake just after starting a soul letter on my computer. *Hi, God,* I wrote, *Jean-Marie here. I'm confused. I don't know which choice to make . . .* The following reply came barreling back through my own hands:

Do the best you can. Choose the highest form of loving in each moment. Be present and enjoy life to the best of your ability. Keep looking forward and taking the next step, treating yourself with respect. Don't make anything insurmountable—rather, mount it and ride it. If it turns out that you don't like the choice you make, then choose again and get out of the way. Standing there and vacillating only sets up a state of resistance. Also, if something is not working, don't hold back loving and cause yourself pain. If events turn out different from what you're expecting, understand that I have a better plan for you. In general, think about what you want, not how to get it; then take a step forward and leave the rest to me.

Other replies are shorter and less immediate. Occasionally I have had to wait months for an answer. In such instances, be sure to check in from time to time, keeping the link alive.

## Meditation

Although there are many different meditation techniques, each assists in stripping away distractions and establishing a direct link with your divine essence. It's a time to remove yourself from the physical, mental, and emotional concerns of the day and tune into your inner spiritual awareness. Not only will you be filled up from the inside out, but in acknowledging your spiritual heritage, you honor the seed of God at your core. To begin, sit comfortably in a quiet place and ask for the pure energy of light to surround you with strength, vitality, and protection. Closing your eyes, turn your focus inward and scan your body, noticing if there is any tightness or tension. Take a full breath all the way down to your abdomen and as you exhale, let go of any anxieties, stress, or concerns. Now take another deep breath and as you do, bring yourself present into the now. Using your breath as a focal point, follow it in and out as your stomach rises and falls with each inhalation and exhalation. As you do, your mind chatter and emotional choreography will quiet and move to the background or, perhaps, out of range altogether. Now, breathe in for the count of eight, hold for the count of twenty-four, then exhale for the count of sixteen. If at first you have difficulty holding to the count, reduce the formula so that it's a 6-18-12 or 4-12-8 composition. Repeat this pattern three times and then pause, listening deeply as you resume regular breathing. In the pauses between the in and out breaths, you may hear the unconditional voice of your soul speaking to you. Lovingly receive the wisdom of your natural knowing. When ready, repeat the pattern an additional three times and listen. Eavesdrop as long as you can and you will know not only your divinity but your place in the world. When it's time to bring the meditation to an end, gently wiggle your hands and toes and bring your awareness back to the physical world. After noting your calm and tranquil nature, thank yourself for taking time to tap into your essential essence.

### Seeing Through the Eyes of a Master

Viewing situations as if through the eyes of a respected master—such as a leader in social reform, a skilled artist, or a spiritual teacher—can alert you to your soul by broadening your perspective. This approach to awakening will require familiarity with living or deceased masters, so I encourage you to learn about those whom you admire. To begin, think of a challenge you are facing and ask yourself, "How would Gandhi (Leonardo da Vinci, Ralph Waldo Emerson, Lao-tsu) solve this problem?" Suddenly you may feel more compassion for yourself and others, or a deepened understanding of difficult situations. If the answer you arrive at is free of expectations, fear, anger, and other conditioned responses, you can safely assume it is emerging from your soul, the essence of who you are. Then plug it into the situation you are dealing with and check it out. Can you see the circumstances more clearly? Does it assist you to discern the truth? Does it present an enlightened perspective? Can you use it for your growth and upliftment? If it assists you, use it, if it doesn't, have the wit to let it go.

### Visualization

Visualization calls upon the imagination to create an inner scene in which personal intentions come to fruition. After learning to harness its power, Albert Einstein said, "Imagination is more important than knowledge." Whereas he applied "inner seeing" to the world of theoretical physics, you can use it to access your true self. To visualize the seed of God within you, close your eyes, take a deep breath, and ask for the pure energy of light to ensure your highest good. Then, letting everything else in your interior world recede into the background, invite your soul to reveal itself in all its innocence, joy, and love. Notice the colors, sensations, tones, or other qualities that arise. Be aware of motion or stillness, noise or soundless, form or formless, time or timeless. Open to its presence and allow it to divulge itself to you. As we learn to harness the power of the imagination, we can use it for our awareness and expansion. If you end by thanking your soul for making this debut, it is more likely to show up on request in the future.

Alternatively, visualize yourself participating in an event as if guided by your authentic nature, and observe its effects on your thoughts, feelings, and behavior. Then thank your soul for demonstrating its attributes. If in either case the inner scene turns hazy, take note of the personality aspect intruding on your reception, put it at the service of your formless nature, and continue with the visualization until you have a clear perception of your soul qualities.

## THE PATH OF THE HEART

An immediate experience of the soul ushers in a turning point: one can either sink back into a deep sleep and reinvest in forgetfulness or resolve to maintain contact with the inner self by following the path of the heart. Poet Henry Wadsworth Longfellow referred to the heart as "a free and fetterless thing" not subject to physical laws. Medieval philosopher Moses Maimonides called it "the tabernacle of the human intellect." A Yiddish proverb identifies it as "the organ that sees better than the eye." While skippering your boat on the sea of life, you might think of the heart as a lighthouse beaming with the wisdom of God, a knowingness more encompassing than any the body, mind, and emotions can conjure up.

So loving is this wisdom once you find it that you may wonder why you ever looked *outside* yourself for affection. Those quests could not help but present you with the personality's conditional loving and its many shortcomings—the rudeness, expectations, jealousy, anger, possessiveness, withholding, manipulation, self-absorption, and condemnation even from loved ones—that leave us crouching in corners, guarded against each new encounter. The unconditional loving of your own heart is safe, for it is honest, accepting, understanding, and forgiving.

To take the path of the heart, turn inward, and employ your fearless courage and gentle strength to remove the padlocks from your lighthouse doors, open them wide, and follow the beam that emerges, signaling the course that is uniquely yours. On stormy days you will be less inclined to compromise your truth, doubt your worthiness, or judge yourself or others. If you do, forgive yourself and carry on. You'll be sailing beyond your previous boundaries, learning from your mistakes, and course-correcting as needed. If you begin to feel lonely or lost in a lifestyle dictated by others, you'll be able to recognize the relapse and return to your true self for direction. If your doubting mind intervenes, tell it, "The captain knows where this ship is going. Please relax and help me live a dedicated life."

Just as a comprehension of electricity is not required for flipping the lights on in a room, no technical expertise is needed for lighting up your life with your soul's radiance. Understanding will come as a by-product of your experience. So risk opening your heart, listening to its divine intelligence, then tacking back and forth along its beacon of loving wisdom.

The secret "you" is powerful beyond belief. So don't wait for some magical week in which there is nothing to do but search for your essence. Begin now, while showering, driving to work, emptying the kitty litter, or gazing at the night sky.

Open to your soul, the seed of God.
Open to your spirit, the breath of God.
Open to your heart, the wisdom of God.
Open to your loving, the energy of God.
Open to who you are . . . and celebrate this precious gift.

# Chapter 3

## CHOOSING YOUR ATTITUDE

*To different minds, the same world is a hell, and a heaven.*

—RALPH WALDO EMERSON

A n elder Cherokee Indian was teaching his grandchildren about the power of attitude through the use of story. He spoke to them saying, "Two wolves are fighting inside of me. It is a terrible struggle between an evil wolf and a kind one. The evil wolf is angry, fearful, greedy, resentful, envious, offensive, bitter, spiteful, irritated, arrogant, hateful, and jealous. The kind wolf is joyful, truthful, compassionate, generous, trustworthy, tolerant, friendly, cooperative, happy, considerate, reliable, and genuine. You also have this battle going on inside of you as does every person in the world." They thought about what their grandfather said, then the oldest grandchild asked, "Which wolf will win the fight, Grand-father?" The wise elder simply replied, "The one you feed."

The quality of our life is determined by which wolf we feed inside of us. Depending on the perspective we bring to it, life can be viewed as a series of positive or negative experiences. If you tend to focus on negative qualities, a change of attitude can shift you into a more expansive state and vastly improve your outcomes.

## ATTITUDE IS A CHOICE

It may be tempting to assume that circumstances dictate atti-tudes, or that waking up "on the wrong side of the bed" sets a tone for the day. However, history reveals repeatedly that atti-tudes are chosen and that people who choose an expansive point of view will triumph in even the most oppressive situations. Often, such individuals leave an imprint of inspiration on others.

Holocaust survivor Viktor Frankl is one whose life-enhancing attitude has motivated hundreds of thousands of people to expand their perspectives. In his book *Man's Search for Meaning,* Frankl recounts his years spent as an inmate at Auschwitz and other Nazi prison camps. Amid the pain of watching his entire family die and the horror of witnessing countless others giving up hope, he uncovered what he called humanity's ultimate free-dom, "the ability to choose one's attitude in a given set of cir-cumstances." As a result of his concentration camp experiences, he founded Logotherapy, a meaning-centered psychotherapeu-tic approach still practiced today.

Author Elie Wiesel, another Holocaust survivor, also cultivated an attitude that transcended immediate impressions from his environment. He said: "I have six million reasons to give up on the world, to give up on any other person, to give up on God, on faith, on literature, on words, and in spite of that, I must have faith in the other person, I must have faith in words, in language. I must have faith in the possibility of every human being to remain human in spite of everything." So expansive was the faith springing from his attitude of possibility that in 1986 Wiesel was awarded a Nobel Peace Prize.

Under extremely agonizing conditions, Frankl and Wiesel chose to turn inward and use their experiences to grow and expand instead of resorting to constriction and resignation. In the process, not only did they deepen their understanding of life, and ours as well, but they shaped their very experience of it. Physically they were tyrannized and held captive, yet spiritually they remained free and nourished.

No matter how insurmountable a predicament may appear, you too can rise above it and receive its hidden gifts. If you know your soul has a plan for you and is guiding your life purposefully, this awareness can be your catalyst. But if you don't, and your attitude filters out the possibility of unforeseen gifts, you may want to expand your lens of perception.

## THE POWER OF SEEING
## AND INTERPRETING

Most often, the attitudes we bring to present-day circumstances were learned as a result of our perceptions and interpretations of events earlier in our lives. If you routinely see only negativity or limitations, for instance, it is probably because you once taught yourself to view life in this way. As time went on, you may have reinforced the perception by interpreting new situations as problematic, perhaps asking, "What's wrong with me? I'm always making mountains out of molehills!" or "How will I ever be able to afford this?" Repetition produces habits, so the habit of finding yourself impeded or insolvent soon became ingrained inside, fostering an attitude of impossibility. Now, despite the blessings that come your way, you still feel obstructed or limited, because you have learned to habitually see and interpret reality through this lens.

Worse, while focusing on your fears of becoming stuck or broke, you can actually create such a condition. This phenomenon occurs because the forces engaged in seeing and interpreting forge a reality of their own, as is illustrated in a decades-old sociological study of twins. The researchers interviewed two brothers who, unlike the other twins in the study, differed radically in personality and lifestyle: one was a well-respected doctor in a small town who participated in neighborhood events with his wife and children, while the other was a homeless and embittered alcoholic. Their father, himself an alcoholic, had raised them with brutal force. Twin A said that at a young age he decided never to be like his father, that he wanted to be honored and to have children who were proud of him. Twin B declared caustically that it was only natural for him to turn out as he did since his father was his role model.

Amid a variegated universe, a person can see only a reflected view of their inner landscape. If you perceive goodness in yourself, you will see goodness in the world; if you feel contempt inside, that is what you will see outside. If you are annoyed, you will see annoyance in your environment. If you notice gifts in your inner world, you will find them also in the outer world. In effect, our outer reality merely mirrors back our inner reality. Quantum physics reveals the Heisenberg Uncertainty Principle, which states that we don't see an object as it is, rather, we see it as we think it is. As our reality of it changes, the object also changes. Like the inkblot test devised by Swiss psychiatrist Hermann Rorschach for diagnosing psychopathology, the sense we make of any situation is only as complete as our inner perceptions and interpretations allow. Through human eyes, we do indeed live in an "inkblot world."

It can also be said that we experience life on the inside and simply participate in it on the outside. Psychologists report that only 20 percent of our reality consists of our participation in events, whereas the other 80 percent is made up of our reactions to them. Thus, while engaged in an activity, a person is far less affected by the task than by the response it evokes in them, which can range from grim to sublime. When the response reinforces a diminished view of a person's potential or experience, that inkblot is apt to reappear on the horizon, perpetuating the cycle of negative experiences.

We limit our effectiveness when we pretend that life happens to us instead of recognizing that our interpretation of it can make a difference between being happy or miserable. Could it be that you are overlooking a special bounty because it is packaged in a way you do not expect, as was true of the man in the following story?

A farmer, struggling in a season of drought, decided to try his luck one day and ask for a sign of God's presence. Stepping outside, he whispered, "God, speak to me," and a meadowlark sang.

But the farmer did not hear it. So he yelled, "God, speak to me!" and thunder rolled across the sky. But the farmer did not notice it. That night, while out in the pasture, he said, "God, let me see you," and a star shined brightly. But the farmer did not see it. Frustrated, he shouted, "God, show me a miracle," and a chick was born in the henhouse. But the farmer did not know it. At last he cried out in despair, "Touch me, God, and let me know you are here," whereupon God reached down and, in the form of a butterfly, touched the farmer. But the farmer brushed the butterfly away and walked on, sad and dejected.

Because the farmer's reality of God was not big enough to embrace a meadowlark, thunder, a star, a chick, or a butterfly, he negated the experiences. Instead of encountering God's abundance, he endured continual impoverishment.

We all face hardship from time to time. But we need not continue to see ourselves as wounded and defeated, or to interpret events as victimizing. We can learn new ways of seeing and interpreting and although we may not be able to direct outer circumstances, we can take charge of how we respond to them. As the captain of a boat might put it, "You can't control the wind but you can control the sails." Indeed, we are more powerful than we give ourselves credit for.

## APPROACHES TO AN
## EXPANSIVE ATTITUDE

Old attitudes were learned and new ones can be learned, too. A useful way to take charge of your responses is by working to greet every situation as an opportunity to live in a state of upliftment and personal effectiveness. Attitude provides the means to enlarge your lens of perception and amplify your enjoyment in life. You will overcome fixations on how things are "supposed to" be and begin to embrace what "is" as you employ these approaches.

## Practicing Self-Acceptance

Anytime you have difficulty accepting your process, another person, or a situation, recognize that you may not yet have learned to accept yourself. Perhaps you are embarrassed by your tendency to procrastinate, or ashamed of your propensity for agonizing over uncertainties. Whatever inner traits you are doing battle with can instead be embraced with humor and grace. But first you must learn to see yourself with eyes that honor all of who you are, as did the young seeker in the legendary folktale that follows.

A young seeker, living in a monastery, was asked one day to renew his vows. But too racked by self-doubt to make a decision, he wandered off into the nearby desert. With each step he took, he judged himself more harshly for the distrust that raged within him. He was about to pass an incriminating verdict when his spiritual teacher caught up with him and inquired about his dilemma.

"I just can't decide about recommitting to monastic life," the seeker explained.

"So how does running away serve you? What is the payoff in escaping?" asked the teacher, grinning with amusement.

"It stops me from making a catastrophic decision," the seeker replied. "You see, at age ten I had an opportunity to turn my life around but blew it. There were things I had forgotten to account for, and I've been tormented ever since. Whenever an important decision comes along, I recall my foolishness as a kid and slide right into self-doubt. Sometimes I feel so defeated by lack of confidence that I want to disappear."

"Don't be so hard on yourself," said the spiritual teacher. "I find it entertaining that you have misinterpreted your childhood decision as a betrayal and created a scenario in which you lose each time it replays." His eyes gleamed with delight as he added, "We are born, we die, and the rest we make up. Next time you invent a scenario, be sure to *win*!"

"How might I do that?" asked the seeker.

"By using your self-doubt to your advantage—accepting it with joy and welcoming the truth it brings.

"Come here, my son," urged the spiritual teacher, motioning the young man to step closer. "Close your eyes and look at your self-doubt through *my* eyes. I am one who loves and accepts you exactly as you are."

The seeker did as he was told. With eyes closed he stood in silence at first, then he chuckled softly and was soon laughing uproariously at the illusion he had created. When he opened his eyes, the painful self-doubt was gone, along with his spiritual teacher—but the wisdom remained. The seeker returned to the monastery grateful for his expanded perception of himself. From that day forth he stood his ground while making decisions, welcoming the call to mastery hidden in his self-doubt.

Like the young seeker in this story, you too can learn to move from a confined scenario in your life to a winning one.

Self-acceptance allows you to experience an ever-expanded awareness of your divine nature and its capacities, inviting your heart to open more fully and interpret your experience from an enriched viewpoint.

## Staying in the Present Moment

More than two hundred years ago, German poet and dramatist Goethe declared, "The present moment is a powerful goddess." By contrast, most departures from the present moment turn out to be anything but effective. The human tendency to conjure pictures of other times presents us with realities that exist only in the mind and narrows our perspective. These phantoms stress and strain our present outlook, causing us to impose restrictions on ourselves and others. Staying riveted in each present moment, however, prevents such digressions and, should they occur, guides us back to our essential nature.

The fastest way to shipwreck an expansive perspective is by holding on to past mistakes. When pictures of archived travesties preoccupy your thoughts, it is best to refocus on the present, forgive the past, and forget it. Yesterday is over, despite temptations to replay it. Let it instead serve as a learning opportunity to advance your growth in soul awareness.

Fear of the future can demolish the present as well. Worries or disagreements about upcoming events often tear at the fabric of connectedness. As one of my clients reported:

My husband and I let uncertainty about the future dictate our interactions. We could have planned for future events and taken appropriate actions, but instead we anguished over them and tried to control them. As a result, we fought endlessly about things that took place only in our imaginations. One recurring wrestling match was over the name of our firstborn son, who had yet to be conceived. My husband wanted to name him after his grandfather, and I wanted to give him my father's name. The negative energy soon overflowed into other areas of our marriage, and we ended up getting divorced before ever having children.

When you feel yourself drifting into anxiety over the future, work with the power of observation to overhaul your attitude. To begin, become aware of your feet on the floor and the clothes on your back. As thoughts arise, watch them pass through your mind without trying to stop them. After a few minutes of observing your thoughts, take a deep breath and notice the air passing through your nose, filling your lungs, and pressing your abdomen outward. Allow for a momentary pause and then exhale, releasing the air through your mouth. Observe and welcome who you are in this moment. Now, observe and welcome who others are.

### Taking Responsibility for Your Reactions

A powerful strategy for educating your mind and improving your attitude while on stormy seas is to recall that your perceptions of other people, places, and things are really about you. This means that the disturbances we experience are an agitation within us, not outside of us. (Our more elevated experiences, too, are inner events.) So if you feel upset by another, see what's going on inside. Most likely what you are reacting to is a reflection or a projection of your own inner state—a discovery that can draw forth a renewed outlook, if not appreciation for the insight.

Reflections can be immediately enlightening once you know what to look for. Others serve as a mirror reflecting back moods, attitudes, and states of consciousness in subtle and not-so-subtle ways that we then react to. If you are inwardly joyous, a person will stir up within you thoughts of your blessings. If you are irritated, he or she will unconsciously do things that get on your nerves. So if a family member is being picky, grouchy, or quick-tempered, consider that this behavior could be mirroring your own irritation. Likewise, if you're irritated by a mate's self-conscious or ill-at-ease behaviors, see if you yourself are feeling embarrassed. Then, instead of reacting to the behavior, realize the mood you are in and the state of consciousness that's coloring your day.

It has been said that when a pickpocket looks at a wise man, all he sees is pockets. The same is true of us all: the image we see in others reflects more about us than it does about them. Erica, a forty-five-year-old business owner and mother of two, noticed that the more attention she paid to reflections, the better able she was able to ward off injurious reactions. She remarked:

I often think of another person as a looking glass. When I see them reflecting back an image I don't like, I've learned to ask myself, "What is that behavior mirroring to me about my own nature at this moment?" One afternoon when my business partner was being extremely contrary, I nearly lost my temper but something told me to stop in my tracks and look inside. There was collision and negativity everywhere; the left side of my head seemed to be saying no to anything the right side applauded. I stepped outside and quietly reviewed my day, which had been unusually chaotic. Then I breathed deeply several times before coming back in. Luckily, I caught myself before I caused any damage.

As with reflections, projections can be extraordinarily illuminating, though they are often more jarring. Projections are those disowned parts of ourselves that come beaming out uninvited and unrecognized. If you have an unhealed issue with your mother, father, or primary caretaker, for example, you may unconsciously superimpose their face onto your friend's during a situation reminiscent of the past. Every glance at your companion will then elicit a knee-jerk reaction as your childhood pain wells up subliminally within you. At this point you have two choices: you can either act vehemently toward your friend and thereby dishonor your friendship, or you can recognize that he or she has become an unwitting recipient of your projection. A courageous glimpse within is likely to unveil an inner picture of pain, a place where your loving can be applied like a salve to a wound. A new look at your companion can then reveal someone worthy of your love.

Ingrid learned about the power of projection soon after she and her boyfriend, Jeff, entered into a committed relationship. Still shuddering from her discovery, she blinked her eyes in disbelief as she told me:

I knew my father's weeklong business trips left me miserable as a child. I'd whisper out loud before sleep, asking what I had done to be so undeserving of his affection. But I had long forgotten about that stuff once Jeff and I got together. I had no idea the pain was still rumbling around inside me until summer came and Jeff started camping occasionally on weekends with his best buddy, encouraging me to spend time with my women friends. I felt deserted and mad, which sent Jeff into a tailspin of his own. My pouting soon turned to rage, triggering those childhood feelings of rejection and despair. Only when I was finally able to differentiate between my husband enjoying a camping trip and my father making regular business trips could I welcome Jeff home with open arms. And once I copped to my issue and asked for his support, he was there at my side, lavishing me with support and love till I was able to heal my old wound.

Our perceptions of others can teach us a great deal about ourselves, but only if we overcome the temptation to react. Maintaining an elevated attitude in testy times takes practice. It helps to remember that other people's actions and reactions are about themselves, so don't take them personally. Your actions and reactions are about you. *These* are what you are responsible for.

## *Distinguishing Your Mind, Emotions, and Behavior from Who You Are*

Distinguishing how you think, feel, and act from who truly you are can help to enhance your attitude and extend compassion in many otherwise unsettling situations. An occasion for differentiating your thoughts from your divinity arises in times of opposition. If you notice yourself fighting to be right, observe it. Ask yourself, "What am I fighting for? Would I rather be right or happy?" We rarely fight for the reasons we think. Rather, a current situation usually triggered an old position. Show your understanding instead. Create a safe place for the old fear to surface and be healed. If you resist, you're stuck with it; if you go with the flow, you move the energy. It can rapidly transform the atmosphere of competition into one of harmony and cooperation. Not only does compassion befriend mental positions, it can lend a hand to emotional conditions, too.

It helps to distinguish your emotions from your essence when you express hurt, fear, anger, frustration, or disappointment—all of which indicate a sense of fragmentation. To be compassionate at such times, avoid jumping into an abyss and blaming yourself relentlessly. When upset and hurt, you don't need more reproach. Instead, remain rooted in spirit. Envision a safe place inside yourself where you can reconnect to your essence. Imagine this inner sanctum offering you constant access to your soul's energy and being off-limits to ridicule, criticism, judgments, demands, expectations, pent-up anxiety, and the pressure to perform. Here there is only tenderness, strength, and renewal of your connection to God. With feet planted firmly on level ground, assist yourself by offering gentle reminders about your divine nature.

Distinction is also useful any time you doom a unique behavior you exhibit. If you don't handle a social situation to your liking, for example, understand that the behavior merely expresses an undeveloped personality trait. It has been said that discernment comes from experience and that comes from trial and error. So rather than getting distracted by the behavior and resorting to criticism, give yourself the space needed for growing and keep your loving steady. A good way to accomplish this is by observation. If you had known better, you would have done better, so don't beat yourself up. Be aware of your thoughts and feelings but allow them to pass through you without criticism or reaction. When appropriate, learn a behavior that you would prefer exhibiting and thank yourself for caring enough to expand.

In all three instances, distinguishing your thoughts, feelings, and actions from your essence conveys compassion through an attitude of neutrality mixed with love. With this upgraded perspective, you can connect with life more wholeheartedly and add greater zest to the journey.

## Giving Voice to Gratitude

Perceptions devoid of gratitude reveal a thankless, humdrum world. With gratitude, they provide glimpses of the sacred within the mundane and further a person's ability to fill up from the inside and renew an uplifting attitude.

The more specific you are when acknowledging your gratitude, the more senses you will engage, inspiring an awakening of thankfulness inside and the beginning of another soul-linking habit. For example, you might tell yourself:

• I am grateful for the opportunity to giggle with my son while reading him bedtime stories.

- I am grateful for remembering to seek guidance inside before answering the interviewer's questions.
- I am grateful for the chance to take salsa lessons at the local dance school.
- I am grateful for the loving that flows from me, with or without words.
- I am grateful for the comfort I could offer my friend in his time of despair.
- I am grateful for my dog's unconditional love and enthusiastic greetings when I return from a long day at work.
- I am grateful for the conversation I had with my neighbor as we nibbled on apricots in the park.
- I am grateful for the red tulips blooming outside my kitchen window.

Also extend your appreciation to others. Take time to thank people for the special contributions they have made to your well-being. Send notes of gratitude, telling them how much their kindness, inspiration, or helpfulness means to you. Or surprise them with balloons, flowers, a poem, or lunch.

Expressions of gratitude uplift the spirit. Every time you give thanks for a treasure you've unearthed inside, you invite more goodness into your worldview and more joy into your life. Each thank-you extended to others weaves another strand of your being into the fabric of life.

## DISCOVERING BLESSINGS

Could it be that life is teeming with blessings and we were born to discover them? Might we be clinging so tenaciously to a hurt that we are missing a miracle? Can a negative attitude form a shield of resistance against noticing and appreciating the obvious, such as stars twinkling in a midnight sky, a robin's nest, a child's first step, a double rainbow, or wildflowers on the side of the road?

The following East Indian folk legend suggests that indeed we see what we have taught ourselves to see, and that there is much more to discover.

Every day for two years a water bearer carried two large pots of water uphill from a stream to his master's house. Hanging at opposite ends of a pole balanced across his shoulders, one pot was perfect and delivered a full portion of water, whereas the other was cracked and arrived only half full. The perfect pot was proud of its accomplishments, pleased to be fulfilling the purpose for which it was made. But the cracked pot pouted endlessly, distraught over being such a miserable failure.

Beside the stream one day, the cracked pot finally spoke to the water bearer. "I am ashamed of myself, and I want to apologize to you," it said.

"Why?" asked the water bearer. "What are you ashamed of?"

"For two years I have delivered only half my load because this crack in my side causes water to leak out all the way to the master's house. You work so hard, and my flaw doesn't allow you to get full value for your efforts," the pot answered with remorse.

The water bearer felt deep compassion for the poor cracked pot. "On our walk back to the master's house, I want you to notice the beautiful flowers along the path," he advised.

As they mounted the hill, the cracked pot observed exquisite wildflowers bordering the path and was cheered by the sight. But by the time they arrived at the master's house, the pot was pouting again, miserable about leaking out half its load.

The water bearer took the pot aside and asked, "Did you notice the flowers were only on your side of the path? That's because I knew about your flaw and took advantage of it: I planted seeds on your side of the path, and every day on our walk back from the stream, you've been watering them. For nearly two years I have been picking these beautiful flowers to decorate the master's table. Because you are just the way you are, he has this beauty gracing his house."

The pot, learning of its unique contribution to the household, beamed with joy. Never again did it pout, for it now beheld its crack as a blessing.

You may not know where to look for the next miracle. But if you view every situation as an attitudinal choice, you will be open to new sights and receptive to ideas you would normally disregard. As a result, you can discover that you, like the cracked pot, are valued and loved. You might also realize that you are the creator of your universe, choosing your attitude, and shaping your experience of life from one moment to the next.

# Chapter 4

## LOVING FEARLESSLY

*If one wishes to be a lover,*
*he must start by saying "yes" to love.*

—LEO BUSCAGLIA

ove is like the eye of a storm. Gales of confusion, loneliness, or heated emotions can be raging in all directions,
yet at the center it is possible to find the transformative
energy of love. We may not notice it at first, since love cares
little for lustful yearnings and other pulls we are accustomed to.
Or we might be looking outside instead of inside for its gifts of
acceptance and fulfillment. But no matter what is going on
around us or how conditioned we may be to mistaken notions of
love, its energy gently swirls within all of us.

Often, this energy becomes more pronounced and makes
surprise visits. Have you ever been knee-deep in upheaval and

then suddenly stilled by the beauty of a rose or warmed by the tenderness of a kitten or awed by the innocence of a baby? In a moment of loneliness did you ever open an old family photograph album and feel your loving nature mirrored back to you? If so, love as the eye of a storm is no stranger to you.

Any time love makes an unexpected appearance, it can awaken us to our essence. Troubadors of the twelfth and thirteenth centuries knew about the transformative power of love. Strolling the streets of France and northern Italy, they sang praises to romance, encouraging sweethearts to feel the fullness of love in their hearts so they might experience their spiritual connection to God.

The inexorable call to love can also emerge in the least likely settings. A client once told me an unforgettable story about a woman named Angela, a soup kitchen volunteer in Colorado. One snowy January morning Angela took her six-year-old son to a neighborhood donut shop for breakfast. As they stood in line to place their order, a horrific stench filled the air and her son exclaimed, "Pee-u!" Standing beside them were two men shabbily dressed in lightweight clothing and torn tennis shoes. One man was tall with hunched shoulders; the other, about a foot shorter, had a dazed look in his eyes. Both were shivering from the cold.

Angela guessed they were homeless and watched as the tall man, clutching a few coins in his hand, set them on the counter. "Miss, will this buy us two cups of coffee?" he asked the counter attendant. She nodded and filled two large mugs for them. In Angela's mind, the men were taking shelter from the storm outside but feeling obligated to buy something, and coffee was all they could afford.

When it came to be her turn, she stepped up to the counter and ordered an apple-filled donut and cappuccino for herself and a maple-glazed donut with sprinkles, a donut hole, and a hot chocolate with whipped cream for her son. Then she asked for an additional bag to be packed with a double assortment of donuts—crème puffs, cinnamon buns, cherry filled, French twists, and glazed with chocolate chips. By the time her order was ready, the men were seated at a table, so she set the second sack of donuts in front of them. The tall man looked up and in a sweet voice said, "God bless you, lady," while his partner grinned from ear to ear. As Angela made her way to another table with her son, tears were streaming down her cheeks. She later told a friend, "I thought I was jumping on a chance to help others, but the truth is *I* was blessed, because I suddenly knew what it felt like to love and be loved with no strings attached."

In that moment, loving became a two-way street. The two men were grateful for the kindness of a stranger and Angela was grateful for the opportunity to teach her son the value of unconditional loving.

## LEARNING TO LOVE

An eye-of-the-storm experience does not have to take us by surprise. We can create our own encounter by consciously deciding to love. Too often, however, we are held back by cultural beliefs or family codes of conduct. For instance, you may have grown up believing that it is honorable to suffer or inappropriate to express feelings. Or you may have been taught to value saintliness and simplicity, or perhaps material wealth and possessions.

Although it is natural to guide our lives by such principles and consider them universal truths, they are actually opinions we have adopted early in life to win affection and approval. As Swiss psychiatrist Carl Jung said, "The more intensively the family has stamped its character upon the child, the more it will tend to feel and see its earlier miniature world again in the bigger world of adult life." If you find yourself confined by past conditioning, bound by old beliefs, restricted by distant feelings, and limited by impaired behavior, you may be adhering to those imprints and missing out on the transformative power of love. It's time to ask yourself, "Do my beliefs and behaviors still work for me? Are they producing the results I want? If I keep investing in them, what will my future look like? Which ones am I willing to let go of in order to love?" It is never too late to release the cultural beliefs and family codes that no longer work for you and to replace them with principles that *will* work.

Just as we can learn to cook, paint, drive a vehicle, perform surgery, speak a foreign language, or fly an airplane, we can learn to love. All it takes is willingness.

Many of my clients have learned to love, and their accounts are revealing. Thirty-eight-year-old Susan, after a long history of unsatisfying relationships, explained:

I got so tired of looking for someone to accept me that I decided to accept myself. It wasn't easy. First, I had to learn to respect myself, which meant moving to a new level of honesty and integrity. No longer could I act dumb and pretend not to know things I was well aware of; instead, I had to get real with myself. Then I had to start being impeccable with my word and not make promises I couldn't keep. I practiced ruthlessly, because I was a tough case. Now I actually enjoy spending time with myself. In fact, I love the woman I have become.

Elton, months after taking a new job, commented:

> I used to enter my work life as needy as could be, though I didn't realize it at the time. I thought I just had to be needed, that if I rescued someone at the office often enough, they would need me and fill the emptiness inside me; but I ended up disillusioned, disappointed, hurt, angry, sick, and overworked. By contrast, I've now learned how to fill up from the inside and I make sure to keep it that way. I've learned to enjoy my work and take time for me. I guess *I* was the one who needed rescuing.

Tanya, accustomed to getting lost in relationships, observed:

> This time I decided not to settle for anything less than what I wanted. I had to be true to myself because I knew how painful it was *not* to be: to win a man's love, I used to evaporate and become a stranger to myself, with no sense of identity. So at last I've found a partner who encourages me to be me. Instead of turning to vapor, I tap into the love inside me and give to him from my overflow.

Michael, a real estate broker revealed:

It took me fifty years to realize that I am the most important person I will ever know. I used to spend my time trying to meet prominent and distinguished people, thinking if they accepted me into their group, I would matter. Then I woke up and realized that I matter, not because of who I know or what I do but because I am me. I am the one I have been longing to meet. I used to be the obstacle in my life, now I am the solution.

All four individuals changed their ways and experienced new results. Yet this was only the start of an ongoing metamorphosis, for as time passed they came to taste more and more of life's sweetness and wisdom. For each, the turning point came when they had learned to love themselves.

Anyone can learn to love by developing a fondness for themselves. This is a love we can commit to. Although anguish or grief may at times rock our boat, we can use it as a wake-up call to return to the heart of the matter and recommit to the loving principle as a way of life. In fact, in times of turbulence we need loving most of all. And who, better than we, to give it? In the words of the Irish poet Oscar Wilde, "To love oneself is the beginning of a lifelong romance."

So begin romancing yourself. Do what Garnet Rogers advises in Susannah Clark and Richard Leigh's song "Come from the Heart":

You gotta sing like you don't need the money
Love like you'll never get hurt
You've got to dance like nobody's watching

It's gotta come from the heart
If you want it to work.

In other words, love fearlessly. Since loving is what the soul does best, nothing hurts more than to shut it down and nothing is as invigorating as letting it flow. Be gutsy, feel your rawness, and embrace the naked truth: you are by nature a loving being.

To start, romance yourself every day—physically, mentally, emotionally, and spiritually. After day thirty-two, if behavioral researchers are correct, the discipline will have become a way of being, and no longer something to think about. When you are no longer committed to others' belief systems and no longer afraid to love, you can be on a path of devotion to your essence.

### Loving Yourself Physically

You love yourself physically when you celebrate your body exactly as it is. Perhaps you have been influenced by advertisers' images of sixteen-year-old airbrushed fashion models that make us doubt our self-worth so they can "sell" it back to us. If so, the next time you consider "doing something" about your unruly hair, undefined abs, flabby stomach, large thighs, or crooked toe, resist the urge to change it. Instead, love it.

Accepting yourself just the way you are can lead to a new beginning. In excusing or justifying a part of the body, we become victimized by it; in cherishing it, we uncover its blessings. Whether it's your stomach, for carrying babies, or your thighs for supporting you in your walk through this world, gently touch a body part you once judged, nurture it with love, and thank it for the good job it's been doing. At first it may seem strange because it evokes a new way of being. But with practice, it will become familiar, habitual, and even a refreshing change.

You do not need to change your body in order to love it. Nor do you need to alter it to invite someone else's love. On the contrary, the more fondness you have for your body, the more loving you can be and the more love you can attract.

You might even find that loving your body may inspire you to improve it for all the right reasons. No longer is it a vanity issue, rather it falls into the category of a health concern. Out of respect and honor for your soul's vehicle, you want to take good care of your physical form.

## Loving Yourself Mentally

Oftentimes we acknowledge and appreciate other people, but do you direct thoughts of acknowledgment and appreciation to yourself? Do you recognize how amazing you are and that there is no one else quite like you? Loving yourself mentally, for all you are and all you do, can boost your morale.

Many people fail to honor their successes because they consider them insignificant. In a research study conducted at a large, respected university, freshmen were asked to write their strengths on the front of a sheet of paper and their weaknesses on the back. On average, they recorded six weaknesses for every strength. This tendency to discount personal attributes comes at great cost, for we end up defining ourselves by—and remaining entrenched in—our perceived limitations.

As essential as it is to express thankfulness for your progress, the attributes you acknowledge need not be grandiose. If during the day you ate nutritious meals, nurtured your children, performed well at work, ran errands for a colleague, comforted your parents, supported a friend in need, watered the plants, or fed your pets, applaud this accomplishment. On less hectic days, reflect appreciatively on a thoughtful behavior you exhibited, a new awareness, or a deepened understanding of your purpose in life. All such achievements signify that you are capable and doing your best, which in turn fosters a pattern of self-support. In calling them to mind, you establish a more globally loving relationship with yourself.

You can also love yourself mentally when you aren't necessarily doing your best. Maybe you forgot to pick up the cleaning, pay the electric bill, keep the dentist appointment, or say thank you to a friend. In an instant, your mind can begin lashing out in criticism and blame, faulting you for not only the most recent errors but for ones occurring years past. Loving is demonstrated when you stop and forgive yourself for mentally judging yourself and refuse to emotionally abandon yourself, like so many times before. Rather, while embracing yourself, support yourself in taking accountability. If you spilled milk on the kitchen floor, saying "I'm sorry" is only the first step. Cleaning it up is next, and the final action involves noting what you will do to assure that the likelihood of it happening again is slim or none. Perhaps you say, "In the future, I will hold the glass with two hands," or "When I am carrying a full glass of milk, I will not attempt to carry a tray of hors d'oeuvres too." When you display this level of integrity, even so-called bad days can propel you into excellence and deserve your acknowledgment.

Appreciation upholds self-respect. It adds to your understanding and compassion of the human condition as well as expresses thankfulness for having the courage and conviction to uncover greater truth. What did you learn that you can use for your upliftment? Is this realization applicable in any other area of your life? What are you thankful for? As your gratitude comes forth, it opens the way for grace to envelop you.

Even if you begin your day at a fast pace and don't stop until you drop into bed at night, take time before sleep to appreciate yourself. Studies show that thoughts arising just before sleep replay repeatedly in the unconscious during the night. This means that the more diligent you are about recognizing your talents and traits before sleep, the sooner you will expand into your authenticity.

### Loving Yourself Emotionally

Positive feelings about ourselves lead to healthy self-esteem. How you feel about yourself—"I'm fun, I'm lovable, I learn from my mistakes, I trust myself"—affects the way you live. Negative feelings, such as, "I'm boring, I'm unlovable, I'm afraid to lose, I doubt myself," if unattended, propel you into infested waters, critically impairing your quality of life. You're much too valuable to hold negative feelings against you by anyone, much less yourself. Ultimately they can squelch your dreams and aspirations.

Feelings of unworthiness are the primary precipitants of emotional pain. They cause us to feel worthless, incompetent, and ineffective; to belittle ourselves; to reject our potential; and to darken our inner monologues with demeaning remarks. Did you ever hear a voice inside say, "You don't deserve to have it" or "Nobody likes you, so don't bother trying"? Such statements reveal a lack of self-worth and a dangerously ailing sense of confidence and satisfaction with oneself.

There is no better means of revitalizing self-worth than through consistent ministrations of self-love. The degree to which you hold yourself in high regard is the degree to which you deem yourself worthy of receiving love. In experiencing the power of your loving nature, you cannot help but feel good about who you are. To tap into your essence and promote a healthier sense of self, follow these guidelines.

- **Keep your agreements.** Broken agreements intensify feelings of unworthiness. Each time we fail to follow through on a plan, we teach ourselves that we are not worth listening to.

  So stay true to your word. If you plan to wake up at 6:00 a.m. and exercise, do it—even if it means catching up on lost sleep later in the day. Each agreement that you keep rewards you with feelings of increased confidence, vitality, and trust.

- **Honor your values.** Write down your three most important values, and refer to them often. If you have difficulty identifying them, think of someone you respect and ask yourself: "What qualities do I admire most in this person? How do they reveal themselves in me?" Then begin to support these qualities in yourself, taking charge of whatever impulses might cause you to undermine them.

  When we align our actions with our values, outer and

inner realities converge. At that point, form can work in concert with essence, promoting an inner sense of connectedness, integrity, and wholeness.

- **Be responsible.** Feelings of unworthiness cause many people to absolve themselves of responsibility for their actions for fear of stirring up feelings of insecurity. Shifting attention away from themselves, they may blame other people for their own oversights, or criticize or attempt to control them. But blaming, criticizing, and controlling behaviors, like raging twisters, leave devastation in their wake—and in this case, the rubble is a more crippled self-regard.

  Instead of trying to change others, look inside. Accept responsibility for your actions, the consequences of your behavior, and your habits of neglect. In addition, find the source of your insecurities and challenge any feelings that prevent you from doing your personal best. Then use these emotions to your advantage. The more deeds you own up to, the more you learn that your actions produce results.

- **Be honest.** We deceive only ourselves. Dishonesty—including the use of withheld, manipulative, or misleading communications—incites so much internal dissent that we become confused. As a result, we separate from the truth at our core and begin expending exorbitant amounts of energy defending a lie. In the end, dishonesty reinforces feelings of unworthiness.

  Rather than reap the consequences of deception, whether deliberate or perfunctory, keep your communications honest. Share accurate information, divulge your mistakes, and acknowledge misunderstandings. Truth telling unlocks the door to trust, beyond which lies the chamber of the heart.

In learning to love yourself emotionally, you automatically replace insults with deserving conversation. When at last you can look in the mirror and honestly say, "I feel good about being me," you will be equipped to tune in to your dreams and aspirations.

## Loving Yourself Spiritually

Amid life's many distractions, it is easy to lose sight of the spiritual dimension. Disillusionment or despair can further alienate us from our essence, leaving us spiritually destitute. The way to break this impasse is by nourishing our connection to the authentic nature inside us. Each time we shower it with love, we take back another piece of our forgotten heritage.

In nourishing yourself spiritually, you establish a conscious relationship with your loving nature. You can do this through meditation, prayer, contemplation, relaxation, silent walks in nature, or uninterrupted quiet time. If you are accustomed to seeking answers from others, begin listening inside yourself for the voice of truth. This, too, is an expression of your love.

In response to your attentive loving, you may discover that others' definitions and expectations of you have little to do with who you really are, and that you derive the greatest fulfillment while staying true to the real you. So put your soul in charge of decision making, and let your body, mind, and emotions do its bidding. Then become your soul's disciple, following its loving guidance in all your forays into the world.

First, German writer Thomas Mann and later, Don Juan de Marco, in the movie by the same name, declared that in any stage of life there are only four important questions to ask:

- What is sacred?
- What is spirit made of?
- What is worth living for?
- What is worth dying for?

The answer to each one, they say, is "love." While living in love, we are no longer at the mercy of forces likely to overwhelm us with distractions, disillusionment, or despair. Instead, we are on course with our soul's mission. We delight in valuing and cherishing others, for we recognize that they too are sacred beings. And like Angela at the donut shop, although we see the devastation wrought by perceived limitations, we can find our way to the eye of any storm.

## A NEW HABIT OF LOVING

In loving, there are no issues, only blessings—so why not make it a habit? Even simple acts of loving can be transformative. Hugging stimulates the pituitary gland, which in turn releases endorphins into the bloodstream, reducing pain and enhancing relaxation. Smiling, an automatic mood elevator, helps to alleviate irritation and distress.

Acts of loving have a ripple effect, as well. Researchers who showed a film of Mother Teresa working with the sick and dying in Calcutta, India, found that the viewers emitted measurable amounts of immune-boosting chemicals. Even the "tough guys" were touched by the healing power of her love. While in a college dormitory recently, I saw a sign that read, "If given enough love, a rock will open." Truly, love can transform all things.

Love, then, is not about longing and searching, or about triumphant exploits in fabled kingdoms. Rather, it refers to the here-and-now gentle winds of a compassionate, knowing heart. You can find it by stilling your mind and paying close attention to the space between the beats of your heart. In fact, each time you become conscious of this force flowing through you, you automatically feed it; and the more you feed it, the bigger it grows. Because loving is our authentic nature, we can never actually fall "out of love," but if it's not part of your repertoire of conscious behaviors you may forget how loving you are. To make it a habit, learn from loving role models, act "as if" you were loving, and practice every day.

## Learning from Role Models

Anyone on the verge of reverting to old put-downs or judgments can instead choose to be guided by someone they emulate. Individuals who exhibit the power of love are ideal role models to learn from. By following their lead, we discover how to nurture, empathize with, and forgive ourselves no matter how dire our circumstances may be.

Countless role models are available. When in doubt about how to love themselves fearlessly, some people draw inspiration from Buddha, Mohammed, Jesus, Saint Francis of Assisi, Gandhi, Mother Teresa, or the Dalai Lama. Others look to a favorite grandparent, an instructor, a special friend, or a pet. For me, my childhood caretaker, Helen, was a simple yet profound exemplar of love; when she rocked me in her arms, I felt engulfed in love's embrace. My client Coty takes cues from his wife, whom he describes as "my teacher when it comes to love."

To reinforce your own habit of loving, choose a role model who best demonstrates for you an uncompromising devotion to soul love. Then any time you face a perplexing situation, ask yourself: "How would my role model handle this? What would they think, say, and do?" As you picture this person in your mind, imagine that you are them and proceed accordingly. In time, you will associate these loving responses with your essence, which after all is where they originate.

## Acting "As If"

Until it is well established, a new habit of loving may occasionally give way to the more entrenched routines of self-disparagement. Devaluing thoughts, feelings, and behaviors can easily creep back into our consciousness, causing us to see ourselves as before—inept at home, on the job, and in social settings. The most effective way to combat these reversions is by acting "as if" we were competent, worthy, and deserving of love . . . because even when we don't believe it, we are.

"Fake it till you make it" is a potent catalyst in reestablishing lost links to the soul. It works because the soul is a fount of unconditional loving. No matter what the personality devises, the soul remains loving, since that is its nature. Even if we cover it with layers of debris, love still remains at our core. So pretend you are everything you know your authentic self to be, and soon enough you will be back in the habit of loving. If you fall, pick yourself up. Falling is part of learning. Life is like that.

For instance, if you suddenly begin feeling shame, act as if you forgive yourself. Assume the posture, breathing pattern, facial expression, and language that you would if granting pardon and mercy. Think forgiving thoughts such as, "I let myself off the hook for having this feeling of shame. I am filled with goodness." After a few trial runs, you will no longer be acting; loving will have become your reality for the moment. Then string together moments of loving until it is your way of life.

## Practicing

The importance of practice in establishing a new habit is revealed in the story about a woman who stopped a musician on a street in New York City. She inquired, "Please tell me how to get to Carnegie Hall." Whereupon the musician smiled and replied, "Practice, practice, practice." Like someone in training for the performing arts or an athletic event, we can discipline ourselves to excel in loving. Practice, trial and error, and a personalized routine form the stepping-stones to proficiency.

To plan your routine, ask yourself what skills are necessary to become adept at loving. Then chart a course from where you are to where you want to be. Prepare a checklist of the small steps you need to take, and complete at least one every day. Maybe your list includes appreciating yourself, exercising laughter, acknowledging false beliefs, practicing forgiveness, cleaning clutter, enjoying nature moments, refining meditation, and developing gratitude. As any athlete will tell you, practice is the key to mastery. Eventually you will advance from rookie to pro to veteran.

We become what we habitually do; and when we consistently practice loving, we become expert lovers. Ralph Waldo

Emerson described love as "our highest word, and a synonym for God." Poet Douglas Howard White portrays it as a "union with God." It is through the practice of loving yourself that you discover your essence, the seed of God at your core.

Also, the more proficient you are at inner loving, the easier it is to attract outer loving. No longer will you be confused about working the sails and rudder of your boat, or about adjusting for changing winds, tides, and whirlpools. Holding firmly to your habit of self-loving, you will be free to follow love's call to ever new vistas of adventure and create an abundant and fulfilling life story.

# PART II
# MANIFESTING
# FROM THE INSIDE
# OUT

*What lies before us and what lies behind us are small matters compared to what lies within us. And when we bring what is within out into the world, miracles happen.*

—HENRY DAVID THOREAU

etter relationships—with ourselves, our family and friends, our career, finances, health, or anything else of value—emerge from the connection we have formed with our soul. Like sculptors of invisible clay, we shape these relationships from the inside out, reaching inward for unmanifested soul substances and giving them form in the outer world. As their contours begin to manifest, we behold in our new creations something of singular beauty and intrinsic worth to us. In particular, we recognize qualities that honor our sacred self and that distinguish the essence of others who, like us, are intent on expanding into their fullness.

Deepened contact with your inner nature has shown you that you are far more than just your form and that form devoid of essence has spawned a miasma of misgivings. For example, you may have perceived yourself as someone's child, parent, sibling, partner, employee, or boss, only to suffer a loss of identity when bonds were severed. Or perhaps you let your financial profile define your personal worth, resulting in escalating greed, defensiveness, or distress. Or maybe you mistook a health condition for your true self and became overly depleted physically, emotionally, intellectually, and spiritually. But now you know that you are not your image, that the misidentification arose out of an earlier disconnection from your inner world. We all exchange inner happiness for massive doses of anxiety when we are busily creating our lives from the outside in.

Creating from the inside out turns everything around, awakening an ever-expanded awareness of our true nature and its capacities, all the while inviting the heart to open more and more fully. The potent energy for these changes comes from the soul's link to divinity, which invites us to tap into sacred space where once there was constriction and to craft forms that reflect its spiritual qualities. In expressing the divine essence at your core, you will certainly be manifesting forms to improve your life, but *you will not be expecting them to do what they cannot do.* No longer will you be counting on them to define who you are and to bring you security and enduring happiness, which can flow only from your relationship with the all-powerful and wise intelligence at your core.

It's exciting to explore the possibility of creating life from the inside out, and it's also challenging. Before going where you've never gone before to do what you've never done, a few precautionary measures are in order to ease the passage. On this adventure, as in any journey to an unfamiliar place, you'll want to divest yourself of extraneous baggage, become at least partially bilingual, and bring along an all-purpose first-aid remedy.

Your most extraneous baggage is likely to be false expectations. Here are four worth unloading at the start. One: *Possessions complete you.* The truth is you are already whole and complete. You will never discover yourself in a material form; instead, look within. Everything you will ever need is already inside of you.

Two: *There is one way to get the results you want.* In fact, there are countless possible methods for achieving your desires, none of which is universally correct. If you stay on course and eliminate methods that don't work, you will uncover those that do work.

Three: *Everyone values the same things.* The reality is that one person's treasure is another's junk. What matters is not other people's appraisals of your endeavors but rather the passion you bring to them.

Fourth: *Prosperity is an outside job.* Actually, outer riches come from inner richness. To prosper, you need only remember who you are. If you want peace, hold peaceful thoughts and demonstrate peaceful actions. If you want abundance, open your inner channels of giving and receiving, since the way in is the way out.

Our version of bilingualism—fluency in the language of essence as well as of form—will further your creations from the inside out by keeping you moving in the direction you wish to go regardless of external outcomes. To establish a functional vocabulary for essence, choose words that differ from those describing the corresponding form. For starters, use *intention* to refer to an inner soul quality seeking fulfillment, as a correlate for *goal,* which indicates outer achievement. You might say, for example, "My *intention* is to manifest more integrity, and my *goal* is to run for public office." Whether or not you win the election is secondary; in staying true to your intention you prevail, because you have become more of who you are.

Another word to add to your essence vocabulary is *cocreation,* work involving the partnership of essence and form, as a correlate for *creation,* work viewed solely as form. Whereas a creation might be a dinner prepared matter-of-factly, a cocreation would be one cooked with love that delights the diners and chef alike.

The first-aid remedy—typically a reminder to turn inward— is needed because new adventures naturally bring hurt feelings and insecurities to the surface. Upon detecting an upset or fear that sets off a knee-jerk reaction, you can assume that an unhealed issue has just bubbled up inside of you. Whereas your habitual reaction to uncomfortable feelings may be to lash out at others, your healing balm will bring to mind the importance of feeling the painful emotions, questioning them, and learning from them. Any time creating from the inside out brings up unfinished business, you have a choice: to react from old conditioning or, growing into your fullness, to move toward a new, cocreative action.

Although different people have different emotional stumbling blocks, turning inward is universally illuminating. Tony, after applying this form of emergency care, uncovered a well of unexpressed love for his wife and children.

I used to blame my spells of unhappiness on my wife and sons, convinced they had brought them on. Finally one day I stopped myself short and peeked inside. Sure enough, I came upon a man still hurting from the fallout of a tyrannized childhood, still feeling like the recipient of endless faultfinding. Now when I'm agitated, I take responsibility for my behavior and, building on strengths and talents, glide into a spirit of cooperation with my wife and sons. I've always loved my family, but only now am I able to show it.

Once you are free of false expectations, somewhat versatile in the language of essence, and prepared to deal responsibly with hurt feelings, you can relax, confident that you are right now in the perfect place at the perfect time to realize your future. Your age, sex, nationality, or past doesn't matter; what matters is that you are a divine seed of God. Your gift back to God is to manifest creations that honor who you truly are. Ramakrishna, the God-man of nineteenth-century India, emphasizing the importance of actively aligning ourselves with the forces of essence said, "The winds of grace are blowing all the time—it is up to us to raise the sail." And as more than one sail raiser has divulged, this journey is not for sissies.

Are you ready to manifest what you truly want? Are you willing to take responsibility for your behavior? Are you willing to turn stumbling blocks into stepping-stones? Are you willing to let your mind and emotions serve your soul? Are you willing to use everything for your upliftment? Are you willing to choose loving over being right? When cross-currents strike, are you willing to forgive and forget? If your answer to each question is a resounding "yes," gear up for hard work and an abundance of blessings.

The next four chapters introduce skills to launch you into a richly rewarding future, including ways to redefine success, cocreate with essence, view all events as learning opportunities, and plunge knee-deep into soulful living. Practice them well and the blessings are sure to follow. As you set sail to create from the inside out, align with your true nature and remain alert to signs of spirit at work in the universe.

# Chapter 5

REDEFINING SUCCESS

*Bear in mind that your own resolution to success
is more important than any other one thing.*

—ABRAHAM LINCOLN

Marilyn Monroe had it all—beauty, intelligence, and talent. Admired and envied by millions of people, this actress grew to become an American icon. By world standards, she was phenomenally accomplished; yet at age thirty-six she tragically died of a drug overdose.

Elvis Presley, fondly known as "The King," ushered into the world a new era of popular music and culture. Handsome, charismatic, and eminently wealthy as a result of his record sales, he became a rock 'n' roll legend. But at forty-two, he too lost his life to an overdose of drugs.

Based on traditionally accepted criteria, both celebrities had for decades held steady at the top of success charts. But their outer accomplishments, fame, and fortunes furnished no inner sense of fulfillment. Marilyn Monroe, as remarkable as she appeared to her audiences, lacked an inner experience of her magnificence. And Elvis Presley, despite an impressive ability to hold his fans' rapt attention, starved inwardly for self-recognition. Others followed in their star-crossed footsteps, suggesting that when roads to success become littered with the carnage of human misery, it is time to redefine success.

## A MORE INCLUSIVE VIEW

How do you define success? Where does your definition come from? What criteria does it emphasize? Does this formula still work for you or does it need revising?

Rarely is a person's definition of success their own. Usually, it is inherited from their culture, a legacy passed down from their family of origin, teachers, or religion. At other times, it's acquired through books, media, advertising, or Hollywood. In either case, we internalize these definitions without questioning their personal relevance or possible consequences. We end up managing our daily lives according to someone else's formula for success and wondering why it doesn't work.

Years ago, I heard a story about a young newlywed caught in a similar predicament. While she and her husband were preparing dinner one evening, he noticed her cutting off both ends of a ham before putting it in the baking pan. Curious, he asked her why she had removed them. "I don't know," she answered. "My mother always did, so I assumed that's the way to cook a ham." The next time she visited her mother, she asked her why she prepared ham by first cutting off both ends. The woman scratched her head and said, "Why, I don't know—that's the way my mother always prepared it. Let's ask your grandmother." They called her grandmother and posed the question, to which she replied, "Because the ham was always bigger than my baking pan, I had to trim it so it would fit." The newlywed and her mother laughed uproariously at the realization that they'd adopted a long-term standard originally designed as a solution to a short-term problem.

Like the young woman in the story, most people repeat formulas for success used by previous generations, no matter how outmoded the methods may be. A woman I know insists that her five-year-old daughter wear skirts or dresses because she remembers her own mom telling her pants are not "ladylike." Similarly, a man I recently met hides his money at home because his grandparents' bank account was wiped out during the Depression, before the existence of deposit insurance. Viewing today through yesterday's eyes, we automatically conclude these are the right, if not the only, prescriptions for success.

When we're not appropriating standards from the past, we tend to adopt those used by our contemporaries, especially the rich and famous. Many women who emulate the upscale appearance of celebrities taking the world by storm associate success with a trim, size 6 figure free of cellulite and wrinkles. A woman whose body is not small, hard, smooth, and young looking may indulge in ultraexpensive cosmetic surgery or other enhancements, such as liposuction treatments, botox and collagen injections, microdermabrasian and chemical peels, silicone breast and buttock implants, or a face-lift. A man ascribing to standards borrowed from the affluent may boast more horsepower by trading in his car for a BMW with a luxury nameplate and by becoming a connoisseur of fine wines. But someone else's idea of a classy image can't possibly bring us happiness since it has nothing to do with us. To arrive at more viable and personally meaningful possibilities, we have to put *ourselves* into our equation for success.

In addition to learning where your definition of success comes from, also identify the criteria that apply. Does your understanding of success overlook inner qualities and extend only to outer assets such as money, career, clothes, cars, a house, a boat, academic degrees, trophies, travel, relationships, or children? Or have you perhaps renounced the importance of physical realities and fixated on inner qualities such as peace, love, joy, freedom, acceptance, compassion, truth, humor, or cooperation?

To maximize your experience of success in life, consider combining outer assets with inner qualities. And rather than attempt to achieve an outer goal for purposes of gaining inner fulfillment, work from the inside out: imbue yourself with a fulfilling quality as you pursue your goal. By maintaining contact with this aspect of your essence no matter what is going on around you, you live each day as a revelation—some of which, otherwise unnoticed, can carry you closer to your goal.

In arriving at her more inclusive view of success, Connie revealed:

For as long as I could remember, I wanted to accomplish two things: to be loved and to be with a man. I used to think that to be loved I had to be with a man. So I frequented clubs even though I didn't like to drink, started playing golf despite disliking the game, and said whatever I thought men wanted to hear. Nothing worked. It took a health crisis for me to discover why—I was going about things backwards. With my health jeopardized, I had no choice but to find and love myself. And I actually did come to feel what it's like to be loved. Soon after, while in rehabilitation, I became good friends with a man who was also recuperating from a life-threatening illness. Now, fourteen months later, we're engaged and learning how to stay true to ourselves while deepening our intimacy with each other.

For Connie, love led to a relationship because that is what she valued and gave attention to. But love can also point the way to a career, clothes, academic degrees, or any other goal you'd like to pursue. The same can be said of peace, compassion, and other soul qualities. Because every aspect of essence provides access to the source, you can regard any one of them as an escort, tap into its reservoir, and let it guide you to your desired form.

Consciously combining your divine nature and your human nature results in a winning partnership capable of leading you to the heart of whatever matters to you. In terms of this more inclusive view, then, success becomes an inside-out reality—the selected quality of your journey plus your chosen destination add up to immeasurable success.

## BENEFITS OF A COMBINED APPROACH

The art of wedding an outer goal to an inner quality provides numerous benefits on the path to success. First and foremost, it allows you to navigate toward your desired asset assisted by an ever-deepening familiarity with your true nature. No matter how many twists, turns, or derailments you encounter, the resulting setbacks will pale in comparison with all that you are learning and beginning to express. For example, if pregnancy is your goal and cooperation your chosen soul quality, the months spent awaiting conception will awaken fertile insights into cultivating your cooperative spirit.

A second benefit of this fusion approach to success is heightened integrity. More and more your actions will reflect your essence, adding a soundness and incorruptibility to your behavior in the world. If while running for public office you are propelled continually by compassion, there will be no chance of subverting your mission by succumbing to name-calling or faultfinding while speaking of your opponents. Instead, honorbound to expressing your compassion, you will be honest and undivided within, gaining power from your integrity.

A third advantage is the field of attraction this method activates. You will find that whatever soul quality you practice soon draws others who express the same quality. If you practice loving, for instance, you attract loving people. The metaphysical principle describing these subtle phenomena is generally termed "Like attracts like." Aristotle, its progenitor, maintained that "like is known by like," that knowledge of anything is based on taking the "form" of it into the mind—an understanding that evolved into the medieval theory of intentionality and ultimately the metaphysical principle you're apt to observe. The implication is that the soul quality we focus on magnetizes the same stream of energy emanating from others who focus on this quality.

Fourth, combining an outer asset with an inner quality eases decision making. When faced with a choice, you can test the options by asking yourself if they further the expression of your true self or if they detract from it. This assessment prevents you from undermining your efforts by taking a course of action that will draw you away from your essence. And the arbiter behind the scenes is the seed of God at your core, keeping you on course so that the forms you desire can emerge from your formless nature.

Last, a combined approach to success boosts vitality, providing incentives to move forward even in dismal settings and on dreary days. Your inner quality, because of its moorings in essence, generates ongoing vigor, while thoughts of your outer goal project a defining image of it onto the playing field of life. Propelled by forces emanating from both your divine and human natures, you enter what athletes call "the zone" and writers refer to as "the flow"—a state as effortless as breathing in and out. The resulting vitality is inordinately regenerative, akin to the jubilance Louis "Satchmo" Armstrong must have felt while alternating between horn and voice on the spiritual "When the Saints Go Marching In." Upon discovering your unique rhythm and pace, you too can delight in the path of least resistance while incubating your dreams.

This combined inside-out approach to success is a bit like companion planting, an ancient style of intercropping that ensured the survival of native cultures in North America. In use today by many organic gardeners, companion planting— the seeding of certain herbs, vegetables, and/or flowers in close proximity—provides beneficial habitats for high-yield, high-quality crops that offer growers security in terms of pest control, nitrogen fixation, weed reduction, water conservation, protection from sun, wind, and rain damage. When two such crops are interplanted, they furnish this type of habitat because of the synergistic relationship they have established with each other. Similarly, when outer goals are coupled with inner qualities, you get to harvest the best of both crops, a yield in which the whole is greater than the sum of its parts.

## A NEW SECRET TO SUCCESS

The old secret to success—get bigger than life and dazzle the world—too often led to happiness with an expiration date. For a more sustainable happiness, we need a secret to success that intertwines dream fulfillment with goal achievement. Here's one that many people find effective: Passion + concentrated focus + self-discipline.

The component of passion turns work into play, a form of recreation so engaging that you do it in your spare time, too. The word *passion* implies that your attention and energy is captivated by something that summons great joy, pleasure, and contentment within you. As such, it has more to do with participation than expectation and pertains to an activity undertaken with gusto, the irrepressible verve of essence. For instance, while it's easy to be passionate about next month's dance recital, passion allows you to be excited about practicing for it. Your passion will drive each practice session, spiriting you on to a successful performance. It provides the strength to sustain difficulty, endure times of disappointment, and persevere with what really matters to you. And this energy within you, which after all doesn't know when to quit, will continue emitting warmth and ardency long after.

The Italian actor and filmmaker Roberto Benigni epitomized passion in all its glory during the 1999 Academy Awards ceremony. Nominated for best actor in *Life Is Beautiful,* a film he also coauthored and directed, Benigni sat in the audience until his name was called to accept the award. At that point he walked along the backs of seats to the applause of thousands until reaching the stage. This high state of play distinguished not only his excitement about the award but also the intense absorption he had brought to his acting.

Concentrated focus, the second component of the new secret to success, involves directing steadfast attention to the chosen inner and outer aspects of success. While focusing on these with mind and heart, you develop a singleness of purpose, which in turn prevents a scattering of your energies. As they become more consolidated, you begin exchanging pursuit of a little knowledge about a lot of things for mastery at your selected tasks. Ultimately this unwavering focus seeds a conviction powerful enough to accelerate the successful completion of your mission.

Nelson Mandela maintained a concentrated focus internally on peace and externally on liberating South Africa from the grip of apartheid. Despite twenty-seven years of imprisonment, he held true to his dual mission, and when in 1990 he was at last released, he forgave the people responsible for his incarceration. Holding on to past grievances, he explained, would negatively impact his ability to replace apartheid with democracy. "You have a limited time to stay on earth. You must try and use that period for the purpose of transforming your country into what you desire it to be," he stated. In 1993, Mandela received the Nobel Peace Prize on behalf of all South Africans who had suffered and triumphed; the following year, he was elected president of South Africa and attained the objective he had established nearly forty years earlier. Undeterred by blame and resentment, he let his concentrated focus guide him to an exquisitely interwoven tapestry of dream fulfillment and goal achievement.

The final component of this new secret to success is self-discipline. In a confusing, upsetting, or unbalanced moment, self-discipline will maneuver you through the most vexing problems. It's made up of simple things you can do to stay true to your mission and mercifully in tune with yourself. As such, it prepares the welcome mat, inspiring you to slow down from the day's frenetic pace and get back to acting "on purpose." From a spiritual perspective, being self-disciplined means being a disciple to yourself. It's about honoring the magnificence of your being—something no one can do better than you, and something others will do once you've begun.

Self-discipline is best initiated with a spoken or written commitment. This covenant you make with yourself may be worded in whatever way is most poignant for you, such as "I am improving the quality of my life," "I will face whatever unfolds and learn from it," "I am watching and listening for signs of unconditional success," "I am allowing my decisions to be enlivened by my dreams so they will reflect who I am and what I stand for." Once it's composed, think of your commitment as a beacon of light summoning you forward and helping you set priorities. Use it to eliminate obvious digressions, detours, and other needless expenditures of energy. Then when you fear isolation, seek approval, feel overpowered, start disowning parts of yourself, go unconscious to avoid the pain of old wounds, or sense an urge to quit, your commitment will usher in steady encouragement to forge ahead.

Wilma Rudolph, a world champion Olympic athlete, was so committed to maximizing her potential that she broke countless barriers en route to becoming the first woman in history to win three gold medals in track and field. As a child, Rudolph overcame double pneumonia, scarlet fever, and polio; crippled at age five, she wore metal braces on her legs for the next six years. While studying at Tennessee State University, she maintained a B or better average while simultaneously working parttime and sustaining her track coach's demanding schedule week after week. Besides keeping up with her team's schedule, she instigated a do-it-yourself practice program. Wilma's self-discipline gave her the winner's edge.

In addition to a potent commitment, self-discipline involves techniques for dealing with obstruction, paralysis, and disappointment. An effective technique for persisting in the face of obstacles is to act "as if" success were within reach. As-if actions galvanize the power to picture and feel your desired outcomes so they may eventually attract their likeness both inwardly and outwardly. While acting as if your chosen quality and goal were at hand, how would you behave? How would you describe your adventure to others? What would your body language convey? If in the course of taking action it becomes necessary to release an undermining belief or attitude, let it go;

once out of its clutches, you may find it to have been the very obstacle impeding your progress.

A helpful technique for overcoming a sense of paralysis is to take one small, purposeful step and then another. Purposeful actions close the seemingly immobilizing distance between where you are and where you want to be. As long as it's aligned with your intention and goal, even one baby step will move you forward and shake loose your perceptions of stuckness. While studying for my Ph.D., for example, although freedom stirred in my soul, I often felt paralyzed by the amount of course work in front of me. My mind would run in circles, then thrust me into procrastination and feelings of powerlessness. Before long I was numb, desensitized, and ready to quit the program. Fortunately, I mapped out a time line instead, breaking down big projects into tiny doable parts, such as scheduling a conference with a professor or buying a book. One by one, my minuscule actions prodded me out of immobility and ever closer to my goal. I learned that small things which are done consistently in strategic places will have a major impact. Even now, the sense of paralysis signals me to take a microscopic step rather than contemplate a giant leap or search for the nearest Exit sign.

To surmount feelings of disappointment while pursuing a goal, view your outcomes in the spirit of investigation. This self-discipline technique—a fail-safe measure for success—involves analyzing your actions in terms of their purposefulness, identifying those that are ineffective or counterproductive, and dropping them from your repertoire. After eliminating what doesn't work, it's possible to discover what works. Irish-born British dramatist George Bernard Shaw once said, "When I was young I observed that nine out of ten things I did were failures, so I did ten times more work." Like Shaw, you can use life's inevitable stumbles to your advantage. But rather than overexerting yourself, simply examine the antecedent actions and remember to implement your findings.

For added benefit, cross-pollinate each outer disappointment with your deepening sense of inner fulfillment. Valuable questions to ask are the following: "How can I use this experience for my upliftment?" "What insight into it might enhance my life?" "How can I turn this disappointment into a victory?" As you gain proficiency in cross-fertilization, your biggest defeat just might emerge as your greatest success.

Overcoming difficulties is a part of everyday life—a perfect testing ground for secrets to success. A person whose formula is geared solely to achieving outer goals rarely feels a full measure of success. And the strategies by which we come to external success seldom help to maintain it, because in the headlong rush for an image or asset, it is tempting to either react to or ignore the difficulties that arise, and eventually cave to one. However, a person whose formula stipulates passion, concentrated focus, and self-discipline is instead equipped to choose a creative action and move swiftly through challenges, learning from each one.

Ultimately this redefinition of success catalyzes an accomplishment like no other: successful people whose lives benefit others as well as themselves. Albert Schweitzer, who combined inspiration with aspiration, is one example. Although he was already a respected theologian, acclaimed biographer, and accomplished organist, he answered the call for the need of medical missions. Led by love, he studied medicine for seven years; then Dr. Schweitzer traveled to Africa with his wife and established a hospital and leper colony. When he spoke, the world listened to his "reverence for life" philosophy. More important, his purposeful life became his message. Armed with your redefinition of success, you too can hold to your dream, overcome obstacles, and cross one finish line after another, all the while contributing to a world more charged with essence.

*Chapter 6*

# COCREATING A
# MASTERPIECE

*It's time to start living the life we've imagined.*

—HENRY JAMES

A life manifested from the inside out is as rewarding and evocative a masterpiece as any work of art. Witnesses, uplifted in its presence, marvel at the mystique, wondering how such an individual was so singularly blessed. But manifesters themselves know the secret agent is spirit and that they are simply mastering a formula for success.

Most of us are aware only of formulas for creating from the outside in. Applying them rigorously, we fill our lives with markers and acquisitions from the material world, then begin battling with ourselves, oblivious to the fact that we've been operating without regard for our own best interests. Even hard-won accomplishments that fail to support our inner desires sound the battle cry. And possessions once cherished end up possessing *us*.

On the other hand, the combination of timeless essence and strategic action leads to fulfilling experiences. These outcomes are not so much created as cocreated—composed in tandem with the divine forces within us. And a cocreated life is equivalent to Claude Monet's impressionistic water lilies, well-executed paintings that evoke the peace and serenity that must have inspired his brush strokes. In the words of late-nineteenth-century British art critic and social commentator John Ruskin, "When love and skill work together, expect a masterpiece."

Stirring the energies of essence into action, you can cocreate a masterpiece of a life. The principal ingredients of this formula are firmness of intention, clarity of goal, unwavering faith, and expansive gratitude. While gaining expertise with these four building blocks of cocreation, you can not only realize your deepest desires but also uncover early signs of increased health, wealth, and happiness.

## FIRMNESS OF INTENTION

Intention assures the quality of a manifestation. Like the radiance of an inner sunrise, it casts the panorama of life in a perspective most likely to keep us engaged in satisfying pursuits. But only when we hold firm to our intentions can they permeate everything we do, imbuing us with endless inspiration and stamina.

Great manifesters throughout history adhered unwaveringly to their intentions. Mahatma Gandhi and Martin Luther King

Jr. were inspired by freedom; Mother Teresa and Jesus Christ, by love; Socrates and Aristotle, by truth; Rembrandt and Leonardo da Vinci, by creativity; and Mark Twain and Red Skelton, by humor. Regardless of how demanding their quests were, the light pouring forth from their soul into their actions illuminated their every step.

To identify your intention, ask yourself, "What soul quality do I want to discover in myself?" Do you want more love, joy, truth, creativity, humor, or perhaps acceptance, understanding, peace, cooperation, or enthusiasm? This question is best contemplated on your own, during a walk in the woods or while journaling or meditating. Simply begin a "soul talk" with yourself, and after conversing with the still, small voice inside, listen for inner guidance.

Suppose you discover that the soul quality you most want to experience is love. Then, begin to follow its call by being loving at every opportunity, toward yourself and others. Luxuriate in bubble baths from time to time, eat healthy foods, learn to be your own best friend exactly as you are, and forgive yourself for harsh judgments that crop up in your mind. To extend your loving to others, slow down while driving and allow vehicles to change lanes in front of you; write a loving note to your parents, thanking them for the gift of life they've given you; speak kind words to the attendant at the dry cleaners and the waitstaff at restaurants. Every time you bring forth loving, take full responsibility for the outcome, telling yourself, "This activity is coming from my essence."

If instead you yearn for more freedom, choose liberation on a daily basis. Exercise your right to decide what clothes to wear to work, what foods to eat for lunch, or what route to take home. Revisit your limiting beliefs and change them to represent more of who you are today. Join a Toastmasters club, if you wish, to practice expressing your thoughts in a prepared speech before a supportive audience. Instead of reacting to a manipulative co-worker, choose a creative action instead. Also exercise your right to vote in public elections, obtain a driver's license, or study in a school of your choice. Engage in a new adventure, learn a new skill, or warm up to a new activity. Reveal your thoughts in a poem, paint your feelings on a canvas, or redecorate a room to represent you. Recognize that you are free to come and go as you please and to choose where to live and how to worship.

In other words, to activate an intention of your choosing, give it your steady focus. Nourished by this attention, it will grow. But even when it is a small beam, each time you activate it inwardly and express it outwardly you will feel what it is like to be aligned with your essence.

According to Carl Jung, while looking within we impregnate our awareness with unforeseen truths. "Who looks outside dreams. Who looks inside awakens," he noted. Maintaining a firmness of intention, you awaken to the palpable presence of your chosen soul quality. Now prepare an inner atmosphere of receptivity so that spirit—the breath of God—can work its creative magic.

## CLARITY OF GOAL

Whereas intention furnishes cocreation with the inner quality needed to fuel strategic action, a goal identifies in advance its form of expression in the outer world. Goal setting begins with desire and arises in answer to the question "What form do I want to manifest—a job, relationship, money, a house, a car?" Like a guiding star, a clear goal defines the direction our mission will take and provides an "itinerary" for the journey. The Roman statesman Seneca wisely observed, "If one does not know to which port one is sailing, no wind is favorable," and the opposite is also true: knowing where we are headed, the slightest breeze brings rewards.

Goal setting starts in the heart, home to our desires. When we look into our hearts, we exercise creative imagination, mentally picturing and viscerally feeling new experiences. As we focus on these experiences, they extend our reality by taking on a life of their own, all the while becoming increasingly clear. Provided that our inner world is clear of impediments while we repeatedly focus on such experiences and act in accord with them, little can stop them from coming to expression. They emerge because goals fed with attention eventually magnetize their likeness in the external world. This is how essence gives rise to form, and it explains why Marc Chagall was prompted to say, "If I create from the heart, nearly everything works; if from the head, almost nothing."

To clarify a goal you've set, look into your heart and perceive what life with your desired form could be like. Comprehend it with all your senses. Now notice yourself participating in these experiences. Manifesting them calls for fastidious attention to three steps: recording the picture of your vision so you can return to it regularly, mapping a strategy so you can identify significant actions to take, and clearing away obstructions to prepare for its emergence.

For me, a picture of a new home in Santa Barbara, California, began to take shape although at the time I was living in Denver. I knew I wanted to move to Santa Barbara; but suddenly I tapped into the desire to buy a house there, a feat my heart told me would bring joy. Immediately I began activating my joy, and once named, it began stirring inside of me. Aware that a manifested goal reflects the state of consciousness that feeds it, I sang Christmas carols in May, skipped down the sidewalk, and danced on my patio to the moon. I recorded a joyful new message on my answering machine, indulged in luxurious baths, and reminded myself to open my heart one more time whenever I felt it closing down. I made a special point of complimenting the health club attendant, leaving a sealed bottle of water with a note for the postman, and dropping dimes in the return trays of pay phones. I even slipped a $10 bill into a shopper's filled bag at the grocery store, chuckling at the thought of her surprise while unloading her produce. Before getting out of bed in the mornings, I recited gratitude statements; on the cusp of sleep at night, I congratulated myself for all I had learned that day. Soon my joy was overflowing—spirit's invitation to prepare for a miracle.

It was then that pictures of my desired home began incubating in my mind, so I recorded them. In the center of a sheet of paper, I wrote my intention (joy) and goal (new home) and enclosed them in a circle. Then I drew twelve lines extending outward from the circle like spokes of a wheel. On each line, I described a goal-related experience in which I wished to participate, introducing each one with an action verb to stir it into motion:

- Discovering a beautiful, spacious, affordable home for sale in Santa Barbara

- Enjoying a view of the Pacific Ocean through its windows
- Appreciating its sturdy construction
- Welcoming its two or three large bedrooms and two full bathrooms
- Cherishing the extra storage and walk-in closet
- Celebrating an enclosed two-car garage
- Valuing a small yard to maintain
- Delighting in a good community and friendly neighbors
- Appreciating minimal remodeling costs
- Agreeing to a low-interest mortgage and affordable monthly payments
- Feeling nurtured, safe, and rejuvenated indoors
- Joyfully sharing healthy and loving times in this setting

I reviewed these twelve experiences daily, all the while picturing and feeling them inwardly. As I did, my essence began tuning to the frequencies resonating responsively inside of me.

Next, I devised an action plan to guide me across the finish line. Every day, in choreographic style, I took at least one step closer to my new home: I studied my finances, determined an affordable price range, inquired into various neighborhoods, then phoned a real estate agent in Santa Barbara. While instigating subsequent actions, I made sure to eliminate whatever might stand in the way of manifesting my picture. I signed a house contract four months later.

Getting rid of possible obstructions, the final stage in achieving clarity of goal, calls for the fastidious release of self-denigrating beliefs and limiting thoughts. Self-denigrating beliefs can recast you as the protagonist in an old tragedy. For instance, if your desired goal is not revealed within six months of clarification, you might tell yourself, "I don't deserve to have what I want," "I knew I couldn't do it," or "I'll never be able to afford this." But beliefs of this sort only bring about the same woeful endings as before. For a happier outcome, replace defeatist beliefs with convictions that honor your essence.

Obstructions forged by limiting thoughts are equally imposing since whatever we consistently think, we eventually create. Thoughts that undermine your capacity for manifesting your desires—such as "All the good ones have already been taken," or "I'm a fool for thinking I can pull this off," or "I'll never know the right thing to do"—block their emergence by instantly replaying old botched scenes. To retrain your mind so it can serve your vision, focus on the picture of your desired accomplishment or form while redirecting negative self-talk into life-affirming dialogue. Also release defense mechanisms that once protected you from pain but currently impede your experience of essence. If in the process you encounter fears, allow yourself to feel them, move staunchly beyond them, and fill the empty spaces with loving.

Having cleared away the clutter of damaging beliefs and thoughts, you will feel lighter and freer. And your goal, more visible within, will be accessible to spirit's breakthrough moment of creation, during which the heart's desire surges forth formatively into the world.

## UNWAVERING FAITH

Faith is the glue that holds a yet unformed masterpiece. Cocreating depends on an unwavering faith that along with a wish

comes the power to make it true. Once assured of this conviction, we are able to be relaxed and detached, with the mind
and emotions assisting the accelerated inner activity now taking place. In other words, through steadiness of faith we cast
the mental and emotional personality troupes in roles supportive of the leading player—the soul.

Whether or not you are aware of it, you may already be har-
boring strong convictions of faith. When you fall asleep at
night, do you trust that the sun will rise in the east come morning? Do you believe that apple seeds will sprout into apple trees,
caterpillars will one day be butterflies, bees will pollinate flowers, spring will follow winter, and planet earth will continue to
turn on its axis? If so, count yourself among the faithful. Past
experience has assured you that these events deserve your trust.

But how do we invest faith in something our senses have not
yet registered and our minds have not tested? More specifically,
how can we trust that we have the power to turn dreams into
reality and cocreate a fulfilling life?

For starters we can look to men and women who have revo-
lutionized the world by believing in their visions. Wilbur and
Orville Wright believed in a machine of their own creation that
could fly through the air. Jonas Salk believed in his vision of a
successful polio vaccine. Similarly, most communication tech-
nology has its roots in faith inspired by personal belief. This is
what led Samuel Morse to invent the telegraph, Alexander Graham Bell to design the telephone, and Tim Berners-Lee to
develop a viable hyperlink system for the Internet, known as the
World Wide Web. It is also possible to invest faith in unseen
potential through devotion to a cause, as immigrants do. Upon

leaving their homelands, many immigrants part with their families and worldly possessions in the quest for freedom of speech or religion, further education, or career advancement. As a Yemeni woman, dedicated to gaining ground professionally, told me soon after immigrating to the United States, "I just knew it was so. Here you can be president of a company." A third way to establish faith in the unseen and unknown is through confidence that circumstances can generally be improved upon. Such is the case with Post-it Notes. In 1970 Art Fry, searching for a bookmark to use in his church hymnal, came up with what eventually became an essential office and household product.

Confidence in improved circumstances triggered the creation of many other items that currently enjoy widespread use. One originated in 1951 when artist and secretary Bette Nesmith Graham, who despised messy letters, wanted something better than correction tape for rectifying her typing errors. She thought, "Why can't typists paint over their mistakes like artists do?" While mixing water-based paint in her kitchen blender one night, she arrived at the formula for Mistake-Out, now known as Liquid Paper.

A similar development occurred in the late 1950s, when the Frisbie Baking Company had been selling pies to New England colleges. After eating pies they had purchased, students would sail the empty tins through the air toward one another until they lost their shape. In 1957, Walter Frederick produced a plastic version of this pie plate and sold the patent to Wham-O Corporation, gifting people everywhere with the Frisbee.

Creating from the inside out, whether through belief in your intention, devotion to your vision, or confidence in improving your life, calls for this same adherence to faith. And like all pioneers guided by faith, you cannot allow yourself the luxury of a negative thought since it might undermine your mission. Doubt fosters a no-win proposition, and despair a downhill struggle. In the spirit of Noah, whose ark saved his family and a pair of each animal from destruction, simply persevere. People laughed at Noah for building an ark where there was no sea, yet he persisted without questioning the results, and so can you.

To maintain steadiness of faith, draw strength from your intention. As you do, your soul's wisdom will further infuse your heart, promoting the sense of relaxation and trust needed to receive spirit's gift. It is the wisdom-infused heart that inspires a pregnant woman to say hours before her contractions begin, "I know the baby is coming." To persevere in the face of utter discouragement, let these words lift you, like prayer beads, to a new level of consciousness: *when you have come to your wit's end and don't know which way to turn, let go of the form and let the essence lead you home.* Under its tutelage your wish will emerge into the light and grace will prevail.

## EXPANSIVE GRATITUDE

Gratitude, the final ingredient needed for a soulful creation, enlarges the door to the heart. This in turn expands the capacity to receive spirit's gifts. In fact, the more thankful you are for all that spirit has brought you, the more receptive you can be to the surprises still to come. In a sense, the portal of the heart through which we give appreciation today becomes the space through which we receive blessings tomorrow.

Gratitude expressed to spirit expands the flow of blessings coming our way by enhancing our perception of it. Each "thank-you" aligning the mind and emotions with the soul's activity stops any conflict between personality and soul forces. United, these energies can then move collaboratively toward the goal of a soulful creation.

Unfortunately our culture fails to emphasize the importance of voicing gratitude in our quest for better circumstances. Instead, we are often taught to focus on what's wrong. One of my seventh-grade teachers, for example, returned my tests with a big red "X" slashed across the page to indicate a wrong answer, never acknowledging the right answers. And the following year when my best friend brought home a report card with six A's and one B, her mother wailed, "Why didn't you get straight A's? What's going on?" instead of "Congratulations on a fabulous report card. You've obviously worked hard these past few months."

It's no wonder that now, after years of similar experiences, many of us fall into bed at night obsessed with the one or two "wrong" things we said or did that day. Or we compare ourselves with others and greedily wish we had what they've got. In either instance, we fail to realize how contracted we have become inside, how much the doorway to our hearts has narrowed and how counterproductive this state really is. Worse, we've lost sight of the fact that getting what you want comes from being grateful for what you have.

In a culture that downplays gratitude, it is that much more urgent to establish a personal dialogue with spirit, grounded in thankfulness for what is—for the many blessings that already enrich your life. To begin, try greeting each morning with an acknowledgment of your harvest and thanks in advance for another day filled with grace. Or express gratitude for the morning rain and clothes in your closet; for your musical, artistic, or athletic talent; for good friends to laugh with and opportunities for contributing to your family or workplace. Whatever you decide on, be sure to include a word of appreciation for the person you are becoming in your commitment to a life of soulful living.

In surrendering to a grateful heart, we increase our capacity to recognize and receive a creation that spirit has called forth for us. This happens because when the depths of our being are suffused with gratitude, we become intensely conscious of the play of spirit within us and welcome it that much more.

With firmness of intention, clarity of goal, unwavering faith, and expansive gratitude percolating in your inner landscape, your outer landscape begins to shift radically—partly because you are registering it differently, and partly because spirit is responding to your dedication. To keep the momentum going, ward off encroaching assumptions about limitation, attachments to how things used to be, expectations of how things "should" be, and trust earnestly in the unfolding. The masterpiece that manifests before your eyes may amaze you, and the one manifesting within, at its source, may be nothing short of miraculous.

# Chapter 7

# USING EVERYTHING AS A LEARNING EXPERIENCE

*There is no such thing as a
problem without a gift for you in its hands.
You seek problems because you need their gifts.*

—RICHARD BACH

L earning accelerates cocreation. On sunny days, when all is going well, it's natural to learn from life's events and further the work of cocreation. But then hard times roll in, grinding everything to a halt. Tears and heartache are as unavoidable as rains and wind. Yet they can actually jump-start a masterpiece or rev up one already in motion, provided that the underlying hardship is greeted as a learning experience.

Charles Dickens, in *A Christmas Carol,* tells the story of a miser named Ebenezer Scrooge, a financially successful but unhappy businessman. In his eyes the world was a greedy place, a perception that had sustained Scrooge's penny-pinching ways and turned his life into a self-fulfilling prophecy. Oblivious to his soul, he had closed his heart to others, balked at the spirit of giving, and refused to celebrate Christmas. Then in a dream one night, Scrooge was visited by ghosts of Christmases past, present, and future—a blessing born from his soul but appearing torturous through his customary lens of perception. They overwhelmed him with scenes of the loneliness and impoverishment sure to plague him if he did not change his behavior. As he woke up, the compassion and loving asleep at his core awakened, too; and in response he saw so much consideration and affection in his neighbors, employees, and only living relative that he decided to celebrate Christmas. So generous were his gifts to them that he began prospering inwardly for the first time in decades.

Whereas Scrooge learned from his alarming dream that he could view the world more magnanimously, others learn the value of changed perceptions from adversities in everyday life. Driven into exile in 1959 after the Chinese military occupation of Tibet, His Holiness the Dalai Lama, spiritual leader of the Tibetan people, said, "One can use . . . certain tragedies to develop a calmness of mind." In his book with Howard C. Cutler, M.D., *The Art of Happiness,* His Holiness also reveals that as a refugee he has been able to meet people from diverse walks of life and spiritual backgrounds whom he otherwise would never have encountered. Extreme circumstances, he emphasizes, causes us to view life from a new angle.

By using misfortune as a learning opportunity, you too can expand the lens through which you view the world, discovering more about who you are and what you truly value. The uncomfortable situation need not be political exile or a bad dream; it could be a traffic ticket, a black eye, plummeting confidence, a divorce, a fractured leg, fear of failure, an in-law's visit, an illness, or bankruptcy. What counts is how you see and interpret the problem, for that determines how you will see and respond to similar events. When you see what you've always seen and interpret it as "all there is," future prospects cannot help but appear discouraging. For instance, if you see defeat and interpret it as catastrophic, clouds of gloom may darken your horizon in times to come. But seeing it as an opportunity for learning alters your inkblot of reality because suddenly you can observe forces conspiring *for* you rather than *against* you.

Many of us have spent years downloading perceptions of impossibility into the mind. The task now is to "rewire" the faculties of perception for immediate uptakes of possibility. Hardwired for this more expansive state, they present an uplifting interpretation of events to respond to. This flow of information gives rise to actions that can be elicited any time we choose to find gifts in adversity or convert stumbling blocks into steppingstones.

So instead of resisting a problem on your journey, welcome it. By responding to difficulties as though they were learning experiences, you just might find what you're most looking for. Or you might begin healing the past and awakening to a life-changing truth. At the very least, you will have increased appreciation for your inherent capacity to cocreate ever more masterfully.

## ENLIGHTENED PROBLEM SOLVING

Like a good story, movie, or play about an interesting character engaged in a compelling event, problems are naturally part of the plot. How the character overcomes them reveals a lot about the individual and distinguishes an amateur performance from an award-winning production. In your life story, you are the intriguing character given a chance to connect to your essence and construct a better life. Basically, there are three parts to your story's plot—seeing, interpreting, and resolving problems from a more enlightened, and hence expansive, point of view.

To see problems through a larger lens of perception, realize first that as you cocreate your life unhealed wounds, doubts, fears, and other hindrances are guaranteed to surface. They are supposed to. Their visibility is a way of telling you that unresolved content from the past is now ready to be dealt with. Otherwise, it would have stayed unconscious, still running your life from the dark and obstructing your progress.

Understand, too, that anything appearing in your life is a sign that you are strong enough to handle it. Mother Teresa said that she did not think that God ever gives us anything we can't handle, but she wished that he didn't trust her so much. Although we are strong enough to deal with our difficulties, the emergence of a buried issue can take us to the edge. At such times, we need to go beyond seeing the problem to interpreting it in new ways.

Interpretation often requires a bit of sleuthing combined with the detachment of a neutral observer. You might begin by exploring a few questions. What seems to be the matter? Who or what is influencing it? Are you willing to take responsibility for your reactions? Are you under a lot of pressure? Then flashing back to the past, search for a glimmer of unfinished business. Has this happened before? Who or what was present then? How old were you? What were your thoughts and feelings? What's the earliest age you remember having had a similar response? What happened then? Why couldn't you resolve the difficulty? Gather as much information as you can, then return to the present.

It's not necessary to conclude that any past event has contributed to the present problem; simply recognize its existence and factor it into your interpretation as a possibility. Simultaneously notice the energy inside you and allow for its expression, working with it as a martial arts practitioner would. That is, instead of resisting the energy, accept its presence. Engaging your heart in this way keeps you expansive and well functioning as you begin resolving the issue.

At some point you will be ready to move the energy forward through physical activity. Readiness depends on the answers to two questions: "Do I have everything I need to take action?" and "Am I willing to take it?" When your answer is affirmative, use your expanded awareness to decide on effective action. Then clarify your next step, set a time frame, and begin moving forward, taking small yet consistent steps toward your goal while manifesting your intention. If you remain unwilling or seemingly unable to proceed, implement the following troubleshooting strategies for enlightened problem solving.

## TROUBLESHOOTING STRATEGIES

Transforming conditioned faculties of perception often calls for a more rigorous adjustment of inner programming. This becomes necessary when long established habits refuse to give way to new ones, preventing the learning that would otherwise occur. For best results, work with the following strategies often and be sensitive to shifts occurring in your perception of misfortune.

### *Viewing Problems as Feedback*

Problems are usually thought of as signs of impending failure. But what if problems are instead feedback, letting us know that corrections are needed to achieve our goal?

Viewing a difficulty as simply information helps prevent the shuddering that arises at the prospect of potential failure. To cure the trembles and maximize your chances of learning from a difficulty, recognize that it has nothing to do with ruination and a great deal to do with getting where you want to go. In the words of Chinese philosopher and teacher Confucius, "Our greatest glory is not in never falling, but in rising every time you fall."

Actually, we must be *willing* to flounder in order to learn. Thomas Edison made 10,000 attempts before designing a lightbulb that worked. He viewed the first 9,999 endeavors not as failures but as stages in a 10,000-step invention. Bringing this expansive lens of perception to his entire career, he managed to obtain 1,100 patents in fields as widely diverging as electric lighting, telegraphy, phonography, and photography.

Abraham Lincoln had an equally impressive capacity to rise every time he fell:

At age twenty-two, he failed in business.

At twenty-three, he was defeated in a race for the Illinois legislature.

At twenty-four, he again failed in business.

At twenty-five, he was elected to the Illinois legislature.

At twenty-six, his sweetheart died.

At twenty-seven, he had a nervous breakdown.

At twenty-nine, he was defeated in a race for Speaker of the House.

At thirty-one, he was defeated in a bid for the electoral college.

At thirty-four, he was defeated in a race for Congress.

At thirty-seven, he was elected to Congress.

At thirty-nine, he was again defeated in a race for Congress.

At forty-six, he was defeated in a race for the Senate.

At forty-seven, he was defeated after a campaign for vice president.

At forty-nine, he was again defeated in a race for the Senate.

At fifty-one, he was elected sixteenth president of the United States.

Lincoln's devotion, especially to presidential politics, suggests that there is no such thing as failure, only delayed results. He demonstrated unimaginable endurance, stemming from a tenacious "I'm not there *yet*" attitude.

Many individuals are tested repeatedly, and they persevere. The typical entrepreneur in the United States has gone bankrupt three and one-half times. Walt Disney underwent bankruptcy five times before building Disneyland. Even sailboats en route to a destination typically spend half of the excursion time off course. Learning what works and what doesn't work is essential to progress.

When faced with a dilemma, instead of letting bitter disappointment dictate a perception of defeat, view the incident as a source of valuable feedback and see what you can learn from it. Is it perhaps time to heal an old wound, or grapple head-on with a nagging doubt or anxiety? Can you consciously agree to seeing the dilemma for what it is? As you do, your interpretation of it will cast it in a new light, reminding you of previously hidden potential so you can further your mission.

Action produces evidence of success. So, objectively observe and evaluate your outcomes. To determine if your interpretation of the feedback assists in achieving the results you want, check to see if it helps you align inwardly with your intention and outwardly with your goal.

### Reinforcing the Lifeline of Intention

In reacting to a problem with feelings of anger, hurt, betrayal, denial, outrage, fear, hatred, resistance, or unworthiness, we separate from our divinity. While caught up in these tidal waves of emotion, our personality digs in its heels and releases our grip on the lifeline of intention. It would much prefer to have us feel the devastation so it can resume its role as master of ceremonies and no longer serve the soul.

After the frenzy, our end of the lifeline is in tatters and all we can feel is disconnection. Miles from the pulse of our soul and locked in old perceptions of limitation, we wonder how we can ever reclaim the expansiveness and joy we once knew. As for our intention, it is a mere mirage on a faraway horizon.

Should you find yourself in this condition, know that rescue efforts are within reach. It's time to begin reinforcing your end of the lifeline so you can take hold of it once again. Acts of lifeline reinforcement overpower the personality and redirect its energies toward soul fulfillment. Simultaneously they reestablish a sense of confidence, helping to open the heart to the soul's mission and providing the courage to move through the dilemma with grace.

To avail yourself of immediate reinforcement, reawaken to the spirit within. Let your compassion flow toward a flower growing in a crack along the sidewalk, or toward your pet, or the stars in the midnight sky. Or chop wood, sending loving energy toward the tree that gave it life. Or imagine a safe place inside yourself—a spot where you can connect to who you are regardless of what is going on around you.

As compassionate energy stirs within you, notice the new awareness it brings. You might experience the warmth of trust, the quickening of grace, the peace of oneness, the stillness of soul awareness, or perhaps the joy of liberation as soul forces are inwardly stirred awake.

Engaging in such acts is far more important than knowing that spiritual forces have been kindled inside you. In fact, you may not have this awareness for some time since the mind and emotions can be slow to register spiritual energy. What matters initially is your willingness to hold firm to your intention, for this alone helps you shift your perspective and take responsibility for your growth. Consciousness follows, transforming perceptions of plight and human frailty into a visceral sense of inner divinity.

With the realization that spirit is indeed "on your side," you will be able to take hold of the spiritual lifeline and accept what is. Then, no longer fearful of losing yourself, you will see once again that you are connected to truth through your intention, the soul quality you've chosen to manifest. "Yes," you might tell yourself, "I am stronger than I thought. I can choose to manifest this energy regardless of my circumstances. This is a lifeline I can count on."

## Allowing for Delayed Results

The perception that a desired outcome will surface at a prescribed moment is wishful thinking. There is no way to know when a tadpole will transform into a frog. For a more realistic view of time, allow for the delayed results natural to enlightened problem solving. And if patience is not your strong suit, turn to nature for guidance.

The birth and first flight of a monarch butterfly entails many stages, none of which can be hurried. The larva hatched from a butterfly egg feeds on milkweed leaves until it develops into a caterpillar. The caterpillar, once grown, sheds its skin and begins metamorphosing into a cocoon, all the while storing energy to reorganize and rebuild its body tissues. The baby butterfly that emerges must then inflate its wings with blood from its abdomen, discharge excess fluid, and rest until its wings dry and stiffen so it can fly away. The slightest interruption in any phase of this process will either delay or disrupt the outcome.

As human beings accustomed to immediate gratification, we are easily discouraged when our patience is tested—an event that occurs repeatedly as we await the results of our new perceptions. But rather than get stuck in discouragement, you could remind yourself of the many adjustments and alignments required by a manifestation. Perhaps interpret the delay as a pregnant pause vital to the maturation of your new problem-solving approach, remembering that you are hardier than any test of your endurance.

To act effectively amid a postponed outcome, support the unfolding mystery. Continue to expand your perceptions of the problematic situation; augment your new interpretation of it (perhaps your plan hasn't yet worked, but you survived); then spring into action, taking a step forward, course-correcting if need be, and then another step. You can advance in wholeness knowing life rewards purposeful action.

## Erasing Judgments Through Forgiveness

Resistance against a problem we encounter opens the flood-gates to judgments. These in turn undermine our mission by building within us defense mechanisms of stubbornness, self-righteousness, and denial, all of which block the flow of soul forces. Separated from our compassionate nature, we begin operating at only a fraction of our potential. So it is that in judging ourselves, we commit a terrible crime against ourselves. By contrast, in erasing these judgments we move back into sync with our essence.

To erase a judgment you may have made about yourself, see it for what it is—a personal opinion you've mistaken for a truth. For instance, if you've recently concluded that you are stupid, this is not a statement of truth but rather an opinion you have formed based on your biased understanding of events. Further, because it is a negative opinion it has caused you to contract with hurt and disappointment. You can erase this negative opinion by forgiving yourself. You might say, for example,

"I forgive myself for judging myself over the way I handled the situation." To reengage with your soul, you may want to add, "I forgive myself for forgetting that I am divine." Then warm up to the situation, reinterpret it, and move forward with this new understanding.

My grandmother gave me the best soul advice I've ever received. She said not to go to bed angry. It's taken me awhile to get the routine up and running, but what a difference this has made. Now if I bring a judgment into bed at night, I clear it by forgiving myself and recommitting to the forces of love. Come morning, my vision has cleared.

## Mastering Fear

Fears of all sorts cloud our perceptions of ourselves, keeping us ignorant of our true nature and therefore incapable of enlightened problem solving. Yet these fears live in us because we have fed them with negative attention. If you sometimes feel paralyzed by fear, try locating it and conversing with it since it might hold valuable information for you. Ask yourself, "Where in my body do I feel the fear?" then determine its location and breathe into it. To gain further information, answer the following questions, "How do I act when I feel scared?" and "What is my inner dialogue?" In uncovering these truths, you will draw closer to your essence, release the debilitating fear, and be better able to replace self-denying behaviors with self-accepting ones for the ongoing work of cocreation. Just as birch trees set seed following the Ice Age twelve thousand years ago, you can bring forth miracles from the numbing chill of fear.

Most fears that keep us unavailable to a difficulty originate in the mind, indicating that we have "thought" them into existence. Further, it is the irritation they cause that lets us know precisely where we need to expand. So as you breathe into your fear to release it, you might think of an oyster forming a pearl from the irritation of a grain of sand; then make a holy place in your consciousness where the fear once resided.

By acknowledging fear, you begin to overcome it. Until then, it can stop you in your tracks and keep you from progressing toward your goal. In fact, it can immobilize you and ensure failure as it did for Daniel in the following case study.

Daniel graduated magna cum laude from law school and was courted by a distinguished law firm that promoted him quickly through the ranks, making him a partner in record-breaking time. But although Daniel was successful at his career, his personal life was in shambles. Fearful of failure, he socialized only with colleagues, whom he regaled with eloquent speeches about his legal exploits. In chance conversations unrelated to work, panic would take over, causing him to sweat profusely; terrified of floundering in unknown territory, he would attempt to impress the listener with his wealth of knowledge. Daniel was unfamiliar with the notion that no one cares how much you know until they know how much you care. All he wanted was top billing in a series of theatrical performances, allowing him endless occasions to flaunt his carefully honed image. And that is what he got, mixed with intervals of desolate isolation. Immobilized by his fear of failure, Daniel had let his brain take dominion over his life, unaware of what a terrible master it made.

When Daniel was willing to see the issue instead of trying madly to compensate for it, he took authority over it. He dealt with his fear of failure, learned new social skills, and made sure to show compassion toward himself and others. Subsequently, in the rare instances when his fear resurfaced he was able to face it, accept it, and walk through it—all the way to his heart's desire.

## Going Within for Answers

Great thinkers from Plato to Joseph Campbell taught that all the answers we seek are within us. The implication is that as long as we inquire within, we will receive replies to our questions, including those that seem to involve other people. As tempting as it may be to seek answers from them directly, the distress is within us. We want to know, "Why does it bother me when my partner talks about our relationship (shows up late, leaves without hugging me, expects me to pay for dinner)?" Or perhaps, "Why do I retreat emotionally when my friend clams up (sulks, complains, gets argumentative, barrages me with criticism)?"

Even after realizing that the problem is our discomfort rather than behaviors triggering it, we seek answers from others, especially confidants or "experts" whom we assume know us better than we know ourselves. But this quest too can be exhausting, and at times futile. The desire for validation and approval can become more urgent than plumbing for answers about why you feel the way you do. Besides, all that others can offer you are their impressions, which might increase your sense of confusion, hopelessness, or helplessness.

Sometimes information gathering in the outer world offers flickers of enlightenment. A close friend might remind you of a similar incident that years ago left you shell-shocked, or a therapist might suggest exploring an underlying fear. But ultimately you must draw your own conclusions since only you can tap the root of your agitation, and when you do your entire body will hum with recognition. At that point you will have not only expanded your lens of perception but also taken responsibility for the part you play in finding the truth.

Seeking answers within calls for quiet interludes of asking for replies and listening to your heart's wisdom. Because of the myriad distractions in daily life, you may at first want to schedule frequent one-on-one time for this introspection. The more often you go inside for answers, the sooner you will establish a rapport with the voice of your soul. Answers may not come immediately, or even within the week. Or you may receive an unexpected answer right away and require time to interpret its meaning and act decisively. Going within for answers takes patience but promises uncompromised rewards.

## Utilizing Focused Questioning

Focused questioning, which directs the mind to seek answers to particular queries, helps program the reticular activator system, a brain structure located at the base of the skull. The reticular activator system filters incoming information to prevent cognitive overwhelm—an otherwise likely occurrence in an organism that receives at least ten thousand bits of data per second through the eyes alone. The questions you use to program this portion of your brain determine the material to be retained; the rest will be stored, deleted, or barred from entering.

In response to your initial inquiry, your internal search engine will automatically ignite and begin locating and retrieving pertinent data. The more detailed and specific your question is, the more applicable the data will be. If you specify a time frame, your mind will sort through information and deliver possibilities throughout the stated interval.

If you are unclear about the best action to take, your focused question might be, "What action step is most in alignment with who I am and where I'm going?" After placing your request, observe without judgment the information that's revealed to you, no matter how uncustomary the presentation might be. The answer can come from a child's drawing, a highway billboard, an article in a magazine, a neighbor's CD, a conversation with a repairman, penguin signage at the zoo, or the forecast plucked out of a fortune cookie. One of my clients discovered his next action step on a restaurant menu. Wherever yours shows up, let it in, lean into it, and test its usefulness.

As you begin working with this form of self-inquiry, your questions might be general. Over time, they may take on more immediacy. Here are queries to prime the pump:

- What can I learn from this situation in order to increase the quality of my life?
- How can I listen to my heart and follow its wisdom?
- How can I lead with my intention today?
- How can I best serve myself and others at work today?

- What can I do over the next month to replace my lust for competition with the spirit of cooperation?
- How can I cheerfully complete the kitchen remodel in the next eight weeks?
- What can I do to lovingly reduce my body fat by 15 percent over the next six months?
- How can I comfortably increase my savings by 10 percent this year?

Focused questioning helps you advance from responding to situations as if they were learning experiences to approaching them that way from the start. Because energy follows thought, perceptual activity marshaled in the wake of a mind seeking answers will soon center on this point of focus. And what you focus on is what you'll get. Eventually your eyes, ears, and other sensory organs will be registering more enlightened impressions of possibility. Increasingly less burdened, you will encounter a world alive with treasures ready to be used to your advantage.

## A NEW VIEW OF ADVERSITY

Daily life challenges us all to learn and grow. Any aspect of it that feels problematic is like a door opening to an unexplored corner of the self. Sometimes it's a place that's just never been visited; other times it's dark, musty, and swarming with cobwebs because it was declared off-limits decades ago. In either instance, it welcomes the new light of awareness and fresh passage of spirit, enabling us to better understand ourselves so we can proceed with our mission. It even intimates that there's no going forward without acknowledging its existence, for it will keep calling us back to our wholeness. In gathering up these corners of the self with appreciation for their gifts, we set the stage for a new view of adversity.

Now adversity draws us forward. No longer are we inclined to run away from difficulties, for we see them as bearers of blessings and harbingers of transformation. My client Ricardo observed how this new perception altered his committed relationship:

> I used to treat my relationship as if it were a contest—an athletic event resulting in a winner and a loser. No wonder it took me a while to see it wasn't working. Finally I woke up to the realization that I didn't want to make my partner a loser so I could win. Now we work together to create sparks and solve problems. We accomplish a lot more as a team than as rivals.

Whenever the spirit of adventure seems to vaporize and leave behind a hurt, whether at the start of a perceived problem or partway downstream, Ricardo currently knows to stop and turn inward. As you warm up to conflicts and other difficulties, you too will be able to expand your perceptions without changing your outer circumstances, lift the veil concealing your essence, and find instant relief from your sense of impoverishment.

Seeing adversity for its blessings turns misfortune into fortune. Now you can know ahead of time that a difficulty, no matter how painful, can guide you to your essence, leaving you richer than before—a little wiser, more compassionate, and more aware. You may even begin seeking the bounty in a road detour, a disturbing phone call, dirty dishes in the sink, a flat tire, a broken engagement, termination from a job, a bad-hair day, or a missed flight.

The world you engage in while using everything as a learning experience is blessed by grace, as it is for the hero in the parable "Truth Serum," adopted from an Ethiopian folktale. In this story, a man searching for truth visited the local elder.

"I've heard of a magic medicine that will allow me to know the truth about things," he said to the wise elder. "Can you prepare a bottle of this elixir for me?"

"To make the medicine, I must have a single hair from the tail of a fierce lion that lives by the river. You must bring it to me," the elder replied.

"But how can I get such a hair? The lion will surely kill me," wailed the man.

"If you want to know truth about things, you must get the hair," the elder said.

The next morning, the man walked nervously to the river, hid behind a large boulder, and waited. After a while, a lion came by to drink. When he saw its huge claws, the man froze with fear. When he spotted its sharp fangs, he nearly fainted. And when it let out a mighty roar, he turned and ran home.

The next morning, he returned carrying a sack of fresh meat, which he set on the riverbank, about two hundred yards from the now crouching lion. Terrified as before, the man dashed off. The following morning, he put a sack of fresh meat one hundred yards from the beast and quickly left. The next morning, he set a sack of meat only fifty yards away, hid behind the boulder, and watched as the lion gulped it down. Day after day, he drew closer to the wild beast until he stood near enough to throw it the food he'd brought, before dashing behind the boulder.

The day came when he fed the lion by hand. Trembling, he watched its mammoth teeth rip and tear at the meat, but this time he did not hide since his quest for truth was stronger than his fear of the lion. Instead, he sang a lullaby to soothe the giant creature while he reached out and pulled a single hair from its tail. Then he ran as fast as he could to the wise elder.

"Look!" the man cried. "I've brought a hair from the lion. Now give me the medicine revealing truth."

The old man looked deeply into his eyes, and said, "You are a brave and resourceful man. You have demonstrated your courage, wit, creativity, and dedication in your quest." Then he shook his head and declared, "There is no magic potion to drink because the secret lies within you, not on the outside. But if you continue your search with the same dedication you showed in getting this lion's hair, you will get to the truth of everything that matters, all the while becoming more of who you were meant to be."

Using everything as a learning experience reveals ever new vistas to our expanding faculties of perception. With each lesson, you can uncover divine attributes still dormant at your core. Then as you cultivate them, you become more and more of who you truly are. Nurture them and they will nourish you. Wage compassion on the sea of life, and compassion will flow into your heart. Wage peace, and a beacon of tranquillity will light your way.

# Chapter 8

# ENJOYING A
# SOULFUL LIFE

*Too much of a good thing*
*can be wonderful!*

—MAE WEST

B eing a southerner, I was raised on soul music and soul
food. I grew up listening to Aretha Franklin, Mahalia
Jackson, Diana Ross and the Supremes, James Brown,
B.B. King, The Four Tops, and The Temptations day and night.
But I didn't just hear the music—I was *enthralled* by it. There's
no way a southerner can remain quiet and restrained after tuning in. It's as if the vibrations seep into our bones and get us
moving, dancing till sunrise if need be.

Soul food has the same impact. I still remember gathering
with friends over plates of fried chicken, grits, turnip greens,
fried okra, and biscuits slathered with homemade butter and

mayhaw jelly. And I recall our parents converting entire meal-times into extravaganzas, making each one rare and memorable, as southerners tend to do. We savor every morsel, sucking the marrow from bones and sopping cornbread in the flavorful "pot liquor" reserved from cooked meat or vegetables.

But you don't have to be southern to enjoy a soulful life. You just have to begin turning ordinary events into extraordinary delights. Instead of sitting back and watching your life unfold, you can make the most of it—composing, orchestrating, and directing it. When greeting situations as if they were part of this great unfolding, you shape them with intention. In response, otherwise humdrum or obligatory events become thoroughly enjoyable and day-to-day routines begin defying the laws of gravity.

In the South we say, "The closer to the bone, the sweeter the meat." Life lived near the bone is even sweeter, for that is where we connect with our essence, home to the sacred forces that give us meaning. By extension, life lived from the inside out doubles in sweetness since it holds that much more nectar. Because of this pleasure factor, a trip to the grocery store can be as intriguing as a good movie.

Theresa, who blossomed into a tenaciously soulful woman, told me:

I always wanted to share my life with an adventurer and now I am—it's me! I finally discovered what I truly want is the freedom to be myself. I used to live my life for other people and outside circumstances, but I've made a breakthrough discovery and now I'm ready to skim off what's not important. Although I used to be nervous about taking risks, I'm not anymore. Fewer and fewer things push my "panic button," and I keep discovering fine qualities in myself that I never knew about. I'm beginning to think my soul has more intelligence than my brain. It sure lets me have more fun. In finding myself, I found a magnificent friend—one I will never desert.

In uncovering your personal potential, you tap into unconditional love and it now holds you in its rippling magnetic field. Since the secret to soulful living is to claim stewardship of this love, think of it as a sacred gift that has been entrusted to your care. If you nourish it well, it will boost your life to ever new levels of enjoyment. All it requires are small yet consistent feedings of qualities that support its growth.

## PLAYFULNESS

Love thrives on playfulness, the elixir of perpetual youth. In fact, love's favorite motto is "If it's worth doing, it's worth having fun doing it." So when you are knee-deep in a project, remember to express your playful nature. Amuse yourself as often as possible, leaving funny messages on your answering machine or taping jokes to the dashboard of the car. Take regular "play breaks," too, escaping for a morning hike, a picnic lunch, or a bike ride around the block, or to skip rocks in a nearby river or swing in the park on a sunshiny day. Lightheartedness reenergizes your entire being, increasing creativity and productivity. If your inner taskmaster, worried about getting scatterbrained, insists on a mission, try this one: seek to enjoy the process, not just the end result.

Play at other times, too. When there are no pressing deadlines, take large chunks of time to recapture your childhood fantasies. Let your imagination take wing. Be whimsical. Indulge in spontaneity and innovation whenever they peek around the corner at you. In times of persistent seriousness, reach inside for a groundswell of contagious laughter. Seeing your inner child dash out to play can connect you to your authentic self and inspire others to join in the fun.

Playtime shortens the distance between people no matter how tense a situation may be. For one thing, it casts off the density of brooding thoughts and emotions. For another, it offers an irresistible incentive for reinventing relationships. Make recreation a habit and you will continually re-create your life from the inside out.

## ENTHUSIASM

The word *enthusiasm* comes from the Greek *enthousiasmós,* meaning possession by a god, or having a god within. When you are experiencing enthusiasm, your natural nature is in charge and assists you with invisible hands.

Enthusiasm is a free flow of energy that gains momentum while proceeding along its course. Like a mountain stream, it can start as quietly as a trickle yet surge into a roar mighty enough to climb the next hill. The exuberance it generates, while flowing through you, adds a keenness to the good times and buoyancy to pangs of disappointment or hardship.

There are many ways to muster up enthusiasm. The most direct way is to say *yes* wholeheartedly to life. But if you're low on energy or trapped in thought, exercise can help get your endorphins rolling; so jump up and down, mop the floor, laugh out loud, or converse with a child. If afterward a part of you is still resisting, assume the posture of an enthusiastic person—standing tall and showing excitement—or adopt an attitude of eagerness. Any of these actions can set your soul's energy in motion enough to lift you up and carry you along in its self-perpetuating flow. Like a surfer paddling into the ocean to catch a wave to shore, we need only exert a small effort to ride into life on the crest of enthusiasm.

Next, just noticing the energy you have mobilized accelerates its flow, hoisting you across all sorts of setbacks. When you get a flat tire, the rush of enthusiasm provides the vivacity needed to change it and carry on; if you fall off a horse, it sets you back in the saddle. Any time you get the wind knocked out of your sails, enthusiasm reminds you of the seed of God residing at your core.

The increased vibration of enthusiasm works miracles in soulful relationships, especially when you direct this energy where you'd like it to go. You may want to use it for tossing ideas back and forth with your coworkers, bouncing insights off of each other. Or you can use it to optimize your health or maintain an exercise and healthy eating regime. If a loved one is out of sorts or depressed, you could focus your enthusiasm on their goodness, allowing them an inward view through your eyes. It is both an act of love and a blessing to see the light in another until they are able to see it themselves. All the while, you are standing as a ray of light and demonstrating the power of being led from the inside out.

## JOY

Joy is the natural state of the awakening heart. When we are joyful, there is nobody we'd rather be than ourselves, nowhere we'd prefer to be than where we are, and no one we'd rather be with than whomever we are with at the time. While in this state of openhearted elation, we see the goodness and divinity in ourselves and others. Even with the washing machine on the blink, the computer monitor beaming out its last yellow rays, and the dog digging an escape route under the back gate, all is well—maybe even perfect. Certainly, logistics can be tackled in this happy state at least as effectively as in a grumpy one.

I like to think of the word *joy* as an acronym for "just open yourself." When your heart is open, no matter how many sirens are blaring in the outside world your joy helps you initiate clear communication and right action. Proficiency increases in this state because soul forces accessed through the heart diffuse fear, the great bungler. It is in states of high-spirited bliss that we hit the bull's-eye every time, or repeatedly find the "sweet spot" at the center of a tennis racket.

Unfortunately, many of us believe that joy is impossible amid hardship, such as financial instability or ill health. The stock market nose-dives and we shift into visible distress, agonizing over the car we'd hoped to buy or the vacation we were planning to take. Or illness strikes and despondency sets in, prompted by visions of ourselves as weak or flawed. The distress we feel at such times indicates that our hearts are closed down, blocking our awareness of the seed of God within, the true source of wealth and vitality. It's no wonder that we come away mistaking riches for bank accounts and wellness for a body that functions like it did yesterday. Yet despite our compromised finances or health, we can open our hearts and when we do, joy bubbles up inside, causing us to marvel at the beauty of a sunset or the richness at the core of our being.

Switching on the floodlights of joy hinges only on choice. It is up to us whether we fight the vagaries of life by kicking and screaming or meet it by opening our hearts. Should your heart refuse to budge, go on a scavenger hunt to see what's happening inside. Are you holding on to resentment? Have you misinterpreted an event and taken it personally? Are you judging yourself or another? Whatever is blocking your link to your heart, release it and replace it with a willingness to see the goodness in yourself. Then experiment with moving into openheartedness more and more quickly. The ability to promptly access a joyous state can add a magnificent power source to your path of love.

## ACCEPTANCE

Many people withdraw from cocreating because they have been held captive by illusions of deficiency. Constantly comparing themselves with others and coming up short, they slip into a stubborn pattern of refusing to find merit in their curly hair, goofy laugh, awkward stutter, and ultimately their very essence. If you have inadvertently become your worst enemy rather than your best friend, you can propel yourself into a new reality by replacing the consciousness of lack with a recognition of your bounties, flaws and all. Then you, like the apple tree in the following adaptation of an ancient Chinese story, will know the exuberance of acceptance that follows connectedness.

An apple tree and oak tree stood side by side for three years in a golden meadow. One day, while watching squirrels scamper up the trunk of the old oak, the apple tree muttered, "You're so lucky. You are so tall, handsome, and strong that you attract animals to come play with you. I, on the other hand, am short, fat, and marred all over by red blotches."

The oak replied, "Don't sell yourself short. Although we are different, you are no less valuable than I. After all, there is no one else just like you. When you learn to accept your beauty and love who you are, you too will attract beings that love you. But if you insist on comparing yourself with me and losing, you can only curse your fate and cry yourself to sleep at night from loneliness."

"How do you know I cry inside?" asked the apple tree, astonished that her secret was at all apparent.

"Because that's what I did when I was dissatisfied with my lot in life. Then everything changed when one blazing hot afternoon a wise traveler named Lao-tzu took refuge in the shade of my branches. While resting there, he told me: 'Be content with what you have; rejoice in the way things are. When you realize there is nothing lacking, the whole world belongs to you.' From that day on, I decided to stop wallowing in self-pity and celebrate my life. If I could do it, so can you," said the oak.

As the gentle breeze rippled through her branches, the little apple tree took to heart the giant oak's words. The next day, feeling more confident about her reality apart from the oak's, she was startled to find that her red blotches were not useless ugly spots but a plentiful yield of delicious red fruit. Minutes later, blue jays came to feast on her harvest, a dragonfly began circling her crown, and a squirrel hid an acorn in a knot behind one of her limbs, all of which delighted her to no end.

When we realize that who we are is indeed enough, others will gravitate to our energetic vortex. Tender acts of cherishing who we are cocreate a warmth that deepens our experience with ourselves and others. It shows up in random acts of caring when you are folding towels or dressing up to go dancing. Reminding yourself how special you are through all your words and behaviors blesses your life with love.

Accepting yourself adds a constancy to the natural ebb and flow of life. As one cycle of your life gives way to another, nothing may look the same: stock portfolios might replace mounds of bills, soothing massages might take the place of wrestling matches, and laughter might become more prevalent than tears. Nature ensures that just as there is no permanent season, there is no permanent condition. Yet amid sweeping change, it is possible through acts of acceptance to experience each new moment as an eternal "now." In times of building up or of breaking down, accepting "what is" furnishes the constancy that furthers soulful living and loving.

## GIVING

In 1985, while visiting Israel's waterways, I was struck by the awesome power of giving. The mighty Jordan River flows briskly into the Sea of Galilee, which abounds with fish and, along its banks, communities of people. Its sweet-tasting water provides a livelihood for many residents. The Sea of Galilee, however, empties into the otherwise landlocked Dead Sea, and there the water is poisonous and its banks devoid of human habitation. With no means to give of its life forces, it has become foul, stagnant, and lifeless.

We humans are much the same as these bodies of water: in giving generously of our soul qualities, both we and the recipient prosper; in instances of withholding, both deteriorate. While giving freely, we serve ourselves because to give is also to receive. And what we receive is an enhanced awareness of the abundance at our core. You have probably experienced how the offering of a soul quality—whether love, acceptance, understanding, freedom, truth, joy, peace, cooperation, creativity, enthusiasm, or humor—rewards you with heightened awareness of an endless supply of it inside. But did you ever realize that you have more than enough of *everything* good in life and in turn feel an expansion from deep within your soul? One way to keep alive the ever-expanding cycle of giving and soul growth is by offering words of appreciation to this sacred part of you, whispering, "Thank you for this abundance."

In giving willingly, we perform a service not only to ourselves but to others, letting them know they are special. On a day jam-packed with appointments, just a few minutes of soul sharing with another relays the message that you value them. Offers of material gifts send a similar message, letting them know how much you treasure their presence.

However, be sure your acts of giving are unconditional, since the "strings" attached to conditional gifts often turn into shackling ropes or chains. Presents given out of a desire for control can easily burden your relationships; for instance, buying a loved one an unasked-for membership in a weight-loss program may cast you in the role of dictator, sparking animosity. Gifts offered out of a yearning for approval can be just as encumbering. While preparing dinner for your family because you think you're "supposed to," visions of them as persecutors may seep into the meal, along with resentment. For the sake of harmony, call out for a pizza instead.

To enjoy a soulful life, reserve acts of giving to times when you, like the Sea of Galilee, are connected to your source, for then you will be in a state of blessed flow. Others will register the fullness of your caring, and you will behold your soul's boundless repository of riches. As a result, you will come more alive and claim your greatness. Martin Luther King poignantly said, "Everybody can be great . . . because everybody can serve." As you serve from your inner divinity with a grateful heart, love pours through you.

You are here to love and to celebrate life's great adventure. Enjoy each moment of soulful living.

# EPILOGUE

*If one advances confidently in the direction of his dreams,*
*And endeavors to live the life which he has imagined,*
*He will meet with a success unexpected in common hours.*

—HENRY DAVID THOREAU

A coho salmon is born with all the instructions it needs for life. It knows how to swim, how to hunt and eat smaller fish, and how to return to its home stream to spawn.

Unlike a coho salmon, we compose our own life blueprint, taking a learn-as-you-go approach. We get to figure out how to walk and talk, adapt to our environment, direct our thoughts, deal effectively with our emotions, develop new behaviors that support who we are, meet our soul, engage in relationships, and cocreate from the inside out. Our best teachers in all these forays are our firsthand experiences, for they tell us which of our attempts work, which do not, and why.

Whether you currently live each day as a revelation or not, adopting a conscious learning orientation in life affords you endless opportunities for growth and sublime transformation. Endowed with the unique capacity to replace former habits, you can take your bumps and bruises, do the necessary healing, and then continue along your learning curve. This means that no matter how unhappy, unfulfilled, or unloving you may have been in the past, it need not be the conclusion of your story. A new chapter of thoughts, emotions, and behaviors can guarantee greater rewards, provided that it is woven from your authentic nature.

Upon positioning ourselves in the stream of life, we discover that risking is a part of the process, and an experiment worth repeating over and over again. And with each risk, we train the personality to support our expressions of essence. So risk being genuine; risk being vulnerable; risk saying yes; risk saying no; and risk feeling embarrassed in the name of freedom.

When we express our spiritual nature, everywhere we go becomes holy ground. So don't wait to honor the seed of God inside you; begin attending to it now, while stirring the beans, repairing the car, filing your nails, or removing clutter from your spare room. Seeing holy ground everywhere avails you of your soul qualities, immediate founts of happiness.

So it is that meeting your soul is not a onetime event but a moment-to-moment deepening, an ongoing rite of passage from who you thought you were to who you really are. Each time you revisit this innermost part of you, you may be swept away by something vibrant you've never noticed before—a potential for more openhearted loving or peace or creativity. In bringing it to consciousness, you become your own messenger of divine wisdom. This is the most precious gift to bring to others because first you have brought it to yourself.

If at any point you wonder how to be your loving self in someone'e presence, follow this counsel: let compassion speak through your eyes as you gaze upon others; let kindness gesture through your hands as you reach out and touch them; let understanding sing through your mind as you send them tender thoughts; let love be your guide as you walk the path of life.

When you live in the mastery of knowing yourself as your essence, you recognize the perfection of your life blueprint—the incomparable awareness gleaned from all the tributaries that have brought you to the present moment. And although this awareness can be shared with others, it cannot be taken from you or leave you bereft of rewards. Abiding in oneness with your divinity while cocreating from the inside out is a one-way ticket to unprecedented success. May you sail in the winds of grace.

# ACKNOWLEDGMENTS

Over the years, I have been blessed with an amazing group of friends, mentors, professors, colleagues, and clients who played key roles in my experiencing, understanding, authoring, and publishing *Living from the Inside Out*. Without their unique contributions, this book could not have happened the way it did.

Thanks to my agent extraordinaire, Al Lowman, who courageously dived into the depths of my manuscript and used his creativity and expertise to assure that its message be passed on to others.

My appreciation to Sandi and Bill Nicholson for their unwavering seeds of encouragement and for being the best friends and mentors I could ever imagine.

Much of the credit is due to the magnificent talent at the Crown Publishing Group—Peter Olson, Jenny Frost, Shaye Areheart, Kim Meisner, Tina Constable, Philip Patrick, and Penny Simon—who demonstrated confidence in me, belief in this book, and commitment to its success.

Teachers are shortcuts to excellence and I sincerely appreciate the shining spirits of Drs. Ron and Mary Hulnick at the University of Santa Monica who are masterful professors in sharing soul-centered education.

My supportive teammates have been a continual source of strength and joy. I am deeply grateful to the following persons for standing forward, sharing the richness of their gifts, and enhancing my life and work—Wendy Garthwaite DeMarco for her generosity; Susan Valaskovic for her insights; Rebecca Skeele for her compassion; Ginni Dreier for her enthusiasm; Cleora Daily for her laughter; Jeri Rovsek for her optimism; Jim Gordon for his wisdom; Tom Boyer for his integrity; Lady Leslie Ridley-Tree for her inspiration; Cathi Norman for her blessings; B. G. Dilworth for his vigilance; Eric Smith for his aesthetics; and John-Roger and John Morton for their gift of grace.

To my clients, workshop participants, and toughest critics who taught me valuable lessons in personal responsibility, the power of loving, and the magnificence of living from the inside out, I am truly thankful.

And finally, to everyone who reads this book, I extend my sincere gratitude and utmost respect. My wish for you is my wish for myself—to practice reconnecting with your inner wisdom, going to the heart of everything that matters, and celebrating the life you were born to live!

# ABOUT THE AUTHOR

With degrees in Spiritual Psychology and Human Development, DR. JEAN-MARIE HAMEL specializes in educating and inspiring the human spirit. She has worked with thousands of people in the United States and abroad, particularly South America, Australia, Africa, and Europe.

Dr. Hamel's goal of promoting integrated psychological well-being took root while she was growing up on her family's farm in Louisiana. Amid a myriad of animals, including an elephant in the front yard, a hippopotamus in the back yard, and two resident chimpanzees, she learned the unique ability of merging simple truths with profound insights.

Financial News TV Network describes her as "a highly motivated adult learner who has the desire and personal commitment to successfully accomplish her dreams." Her dream of enjoying a more purposeful, joyful, and authentic life led to her exploration and application of living from the inside out.

Dr. Jean-Marie Hamel resides in Santa Barbara, California.

For information about her speaking engagements, workshops, or one-on-one coaching sessions, please visit her website: jeanmariehamel.com.